Praise for *Thri*

"There are victims of childhoo[...]
academic authorities on childhood sexua[...]
novelist and poet Denise Bossarte, who was molested by her
grandfather, bridges the gap in this stunning book and lays claim to
her right to be an authority."

    —Susan Brownmiller, author of *Against Our Will: Men, Women and
    Rape.*

"*Thriving* vividly captures the confusing impact of incest on a
developing girl and achieves a needed goal for a book about incest—
she takes the shame out. Through her candid account of what she
endured and her sharing of the concrete steps she took in the
aftermath, Bossarte reveals how she came to understand herself and
the world, giving the reader both guidance and permission to do the
same. Highly recommended."

    —Patricia A. O'Gorman, PhD, psychologist, speaker, and author of
    *Healing Trauma Through Self-Parenting, The 12 Steps to Self-Parenting
    for Adult Children*, and *The Resilient Woman*.

"This book is an impressive addition to the self-help literature,
especially for those who have suffered incestuous abuse, with all its
additional complications. Denise Bossarte is forthright in describing
her abuse at the hands of her grandfather and especially its negative
consequences on her identity, sense of self, and ability to trust others.
The focus of the book is on how she reversed the trajectory of her life
and learned to thrive. She offers a wide variety of methods and
resources to encourage and assist others, interspersed with sage
comments and advice. Her poetry is especially poignant and
inspirational. Brava!"

    —Christine A. Courtois, PhD, ABPP – consultant/trainer, trauma
    psychology and trauma treatment, and author of *Healing the Incest*

Wound: Adult Survivors in Therapy, and *It's Not You, It's What Happened to You: Complex Trauma and Treatment*

"With sensitivity, caring, and compassion, Bossarte reflects on her experiences and the many helpful and enriching pathways she's traveled on her profound journey of healing from childhood sexual abuse into thriving adulthood. She's created a rich, resource-filled and practical guidebook for both those beginning that same journey as well as for those further along who are yearning to move beyond survivor-ship into thriver-ship. Throughout, there are cautions when potentially triggering material is ahead."

—Robyn L Posin, PhD author of *Choosing Gentleness: Opening Our Hearts to All the Ways We Feel and Are in Every Moment, Go Only As Fast*, and *Tenderly Embracing All the Ways That I Feel and Am*

"In *Thriving after Sexual Abuse*, Denise Bossarte has written the ultimate comprehensive guide for survivors and for those of us who care for them. I believe Dr. Bossarte's book covers what I call the mental health trinity of the healing process when she addresses the mental, emotional, and physical aspect of recovering and surviving sexual abuse. As a clinical psychotherapist, I believe every mental health professional would benefit from having *Thriving After Sexual Abuse* on their resource list."

—Julia A. Boyd, MEd, LMHC, author of *In the Company of My Sisters: Black Women and Self-Esteem, Girlfriend to Girlfriend: Everyday Wisdom and Affirmations from the Sister Circle*, and *Can I Get a Witness: Black Women and Depression.*

"Seldom do you get a book that is both wildly practical and ferociously courageous. Dr. Bossarte somehow manages both in this important work. With kindness and strength, she faces the deepest heartache of abuse and keeps moving toward an unabashed healing by not denying the violence but truly facing it head on and learning what it means to thrive!"

—Andrew J. Bauman, therapist, cofounder & director of the Christian Counseling Center: For Sexual Health & Trauma (CCC), author of *Stumbling toward Wholeness: How the Love of God Changes Us* and *The Sexually Healthy Man: Essays on Spirituality, Sexuality, & Restoration*

"Denise Bossarte writes skillfully and courageously in crafting this memoir and guide. It takes us through her difficult but necessary journey to better understand the experience of victims of sexual abuse, and then crafts a step-by-step path to recovery, one that is respectful of experience, comprehensive in context, and deeply relational in essence. Victims will be inspired, and those of us who care will be educated. For those who've experienced abuse, Denise's story outlines a path forward to authentic self-acceptance, recovery, and triumph, and for others, whether allies or treaters, this book should be required reading."

— Blaise Aguirre, MD, medical director of 3East Continuum of Care, McLean Hospital, assistant professor in psychiatry, Harvard Medical School Department of Psychiatry, coauthor of *Fighting Back: What an Olympic Champion's Story Can Teach Us about Recognizing and Preventing Child Sexual Abuse—and Helping Kids Recover*

"Denise Bossarte's practical book for survivors of sexual abuse is written in a way that feels like talking with a wise friend. Thoughtful and thought-provoking questions guide a process of self-exploration and the discussion of her personal experiences coming to terms with abuse and entitlement to thrive enriches the process."

—Laurie Leitch, PhD, director, Threshold GlobalWorks, neuroscience-based skills to amplify natural resilience

"As survivors of abuse, we need to know we are not alone and that there are others out there who have not only survived, but who are thriving in a life they love. Denise Bossarte courageously offers us her survivor story, full of honesty, personal experiences, and the healing tools and practices that have supported her growth and helped her find joy and freedom along her journey."

—Nicole Braddock Bromley, founder of OneVOICE and OneVOICE4freedom, host of The OneVOICE Podcast, author of HUSH and director of UNLEASH virtual survivor support groups

"Denise talks openly and candidly about her abuse. She describes precisely the effects and feelings of abuse that happen immediately when the abuse starts. She is honest with the reader about how hard and terrifying the healing journey can be, while laying out a proven path of steps to recovery. These steps have worked for her as well as many other survivors who have walked this healing journey. Most importantly, her book is written from a first-person perspective, which makes it very reader-friendly."

—Randy Boyd, CADC II, pastor, author Healing the Wounded Child Within, 30 Day Devotional to Wholeness, 7-Day Challenge

"Thriving After Sexual Abuse by Denise Bossarte is a timeless, inspiring, and intimate healing narrative for sexual assault survivors, their partners, and support professionals open to trying practical steps toward thriving beyond trauma histories. The key to Denise's healing approach throughout this book encourages readers to "find what you need at your own pace," as well as her remarkably intimate poetry and lists of creative outlets for finding personal joy."

—Hank Estrada, pioneer male survivor spokesman, author, artist; Prevention, Leadership, Education, Assistance (P.L.E.A), the National Organization for Male Survivors

Quarterfinalist in the 2019 BookLife Prize Nonfiction Contest, Self-help Category (unpublished manuscript)

Idea/Concept: In an eloquent and empathetic manual, Bossarte recounts her own traumatic experience with childhood sexual abuse before laying out a blueprint for other survivors to heal themselves. Emphasizing that the work is not a "tell-all" of her own abuse, but instead a helping resource, Bossarte offers tangible strategies for readers to reclaim their lives and move forward.

Prose: Bossarte writes with fierce candor as she shares her memories of her abuse and its enduring impact on her life. She freely expresses her rage, her feelings of confusion and loathing, and how the experience of abuse forever changed her. The book's tone transitions into one more pragmatic, as the author shares tips and suggestions for readers to seek help, self-reflect, and pursue healing through a range of activities.

Originality: Books devoted to the topic of sexual abuse aren't uncommon. Bossarte's book is unique in that the author comes at her awareness through personal experience, which she openly shares with readers. Bossarte's integration of questions for self-reflection invites readers to be proactive in their own healing process.

Execution: Bossarte's advice for abuse survivors ranges from heartfelt assurances to more concrete suggestions for working through particular challenges. Bossarte gently instructs readers on confronting an abuser or family member who had knowledge of the abuse; dealing with triggering circumstances; and piecing together fractured memories, among other topics.

"Thoughtful and sensitively written advice on how to cope with the aftermath of sexual abuse. Highly recommended!" A "Wishing Shelf" Book Review

A 'Wishing Shelf' Book Review

Being a medical doctor, I often try to help people who have suffered from sexual abuse. Although it saddens me to know such terrible things happen, I'm always heartened when I read a book of this nature which offers such a positive way forward for victims. In *Thriving After Sexual Abuse*, the author, a victim herself, offers constructive advice in terms of seeking help and ways in which victims can find future happiness and fulfillment. I thought this to be a very thoughtfully-written book, focusing not so much on the abuse itself, but on how victim can rise above it and reclaim his or her self-worth.

Sadly, anybody can suffer from sexual abuse. So, for a book of this nature, accessibility is vital. Thankfully, the author of this book not only has a lot to say and a lot of help to offer, but she also happens to be an excellent writer. She knows how to put across a message, and to do so succinctly and without any fluff.

I would be happy to recommend this book to anybody who works with victims of abuse, sexual or otherwise. I think it offers positive, practical advice which health workers would find most helpful when trying to find ways of assisting victims. Also, I think any victim of sexual abuse would find this book not only supportive, but also a shining light of hope that things can get better.

"Denise Bossarte's new book, Thriving After Sexual Abuse, is painful, helpful, and hopeful; painful in the frank telling of sexual abuse at the hands of her grandfather; helpful in its detailed, step-by-step guide to acknowledging the problem and what to do about it; and hopeful in that Bossarte truly is thriving now and wants the same for you. I know; I've been on a similar journey and wish I had had this book when I was floundering. Bossarte is not a therapist, but you can trust her as a reliable guide to direct you to your next step on your path to healing."

—Joanne Spence, BSW, MA, C-IAYT, yoga teacher, and author of *Trauma-Informed Yoga: A Toolbox for Therapists: 47 Simple Practices to Calm, Balance, and Restore the Nervous System*

"The things I admire the most about Denise are her strength and how she has used her wisdom and knowledge to help and empower others to be thrivers just like she is. Her book is beautifully written and can be used as a personal guide and mentor, and I would recommend it to anybody looking to heal."

—Anu Verma, a fellow survivor and author of Victim 2 Victor book and podcast show

"Denise Bossarte's book *Thriving After Sexual Abuse* speaks from the heart about her childhood experience with sexual abuse. Her book is written in an easy-to-read format and provides a wealth of information for sexual abuse survivors. As a mental health professional, I believe this is an incredibly valuable resource to have on my shelf of go-to books when working with clients. I highly recommend *Thriving After Sexual Abuse*."

—Julie Burden, MEd, LPC

"Denise Bossarte courageously shares her experience of healing from childhood sexual abuse in a way that is vulnerable and accessible. In openly sharing her journey, she provides a rich resource for others embarking on, or in the midst of, their own journeys toward recovering with childhood sexual abuse."

—D. Skeetz Edinger, MS, LMFT, family therapist

"5 stars!! Denise's book is a must read for anyone who has been though sexual trauma. Her insight and methods for overcoming such a tumultuous life event are enlightening."

—Tiffany Barnes, survivor, podcast host of Speak Loud, and founder of S.H.A.R.E.

"Like sitting down to coffee with an understanding friend, reading Denise Bossarte's book offers companionship on the healing journey after sexual abuse. Drawing from personal experience and research, she provides a trail guide filled with creative healing tools, mindful reflections, and valuable resources that empower. You are not alone. This book can help you create a personalized path that takes you from surviving sexual abuse to thriving in your life."

—Rev. Jeniffer Hutchins, founding minister Unity Arts Ministry

"Denise Bossarte offers a straightforward, practical guide to anyone who has experienced sexual abuse and is exploring the first and next steps in addressing the personal and extended pain and hopelessness that this recognition can bring. This is a practical book, born of her personal trauma and struggles to deal with it. The solutions she offers will apply to many, if not all, of those seeking a way through these particular hells and offer a step-by-step guide toward healing."

—Jake Lorfing, psychiatric RN (retired), meditation instructor

"Like a trusted friend, Denise takes you gently by the hand and guides you step by step on your path to healing from sexual abuse. Her gift of organization makes the book easy to read. At the end of each chapter, she encourages you and leads you to take action as you move closer toward wellness. By learning what has helped her transition to a life of thriving, you can create your own plan by incorporating what resonates with you. This book will bring comfort and guidance. Learn from Denise. She has paved the way for you."

--Kristin Fitzgerald Gutweiler, PA, yoga instructor

"I recommend Denise Bossarte's book *Thriving After Sexual Abuse* to anyone who has gone through this experience. Denise offers her readers a smooth, compassionate and honest read on a difficult subject. She is genuinely interested in assisting others who share her experience so that they can heal and create the life they desire. This book offers helpful and practical suggestions for how a person surviving sexual abuse can begin and stay on the course of their personal healing journey. This information is coupled with simple and effective worksheets to keep the reader on track and focused. *A Huge Thank You* to Denise and her very special and important book."

—Selise Stewart, yoga teacher

"Denise Bossarte shares her inspiring journey of healing while assisting readers on their own journeys. Through meditation and other enriching methods, she discovered a space between her negative thinking and who she really was—whole and complete. Her path from Survivor to Thriver is filled with curiosity and creativity."

—Celeste Budwit-Hunter, meditation instructor

THRIVING
AFTER SEXUAL
ABUSE

Break Your Bondage to the Past

and Live a Life You Love

Denise Bossarte

To a living life you love!

Trigger Warning: This book includes material around topics of childhood sexual abuse, suicidal ideation, and eating disorders. I acknowledge that this content may be difficult. I also encourage you to care for your safety and well-being.

Published in the United States by Passion for Life Press.
info@denisebossartebooks.com

Interior design © 2017 BookDesignTemplates.com

ISBN 978-1-7370160-0-7

Cover design by Zelena CoverBookDesigns
Editing by Candace Johnson, Change It Up Editing

Questions in Individual Therapy chapter are based on information from the following:

- American Psychological Association www.apa.org,
- American Counseling Association www.counseling.org,
- Association for Marriage and Family Therapy (AAMFT) aamft.org, and
- WINGS foundation www.wingsfound.org.
- https://www.apa.org/helpcenter/choose-therapist.aspx
- https://www.wingsfound.org/find-the-right-therapist/
- Adult Survivors of Child Abuse (ASCA) http://www.ascasup-port.org/_downloads/TherapistSearchResourceGuide.pdf

To my husband—
who always saw the real me,
no matter how deep I tried to hide her.

To Peggy—
No matter what life threw at you,
you always met it with grace, compassion and authenticity.
You are an inspiration.

DISCLAIMERS

The material contained on this book is provided for general information purposes only. The content is not intended to be a substitute for professional advice, diagnosis, or treatment, or individualized mental health therapy provided in person by a professional.

Always seek the advice of your mental health professional or other qualified health provider with any questions you may have regarding your situation.

Always consult your physician before starting any physical activity.

"I AM" MANTRA

I AM STRONG

I AM BEAUTIFUL

I AM WORTHY OF LOVE

*I AM NOT RESPONSIBLE FOR
WHAT HAPPENED TO ME*

*I DO NOT LET THE PAST DEFINE ME;
I DEFINE MYSELF*

Contents

Foreword

By Beverly Engel

Beverly Engel, LMFT is considered one of the world's leading experts on abuse recovery, and is the author of 23 self-help books, including It Wasn't Your Fault: Freeing Yourself from the Shame of Childhood Abuse with the Power of Self-Compassion.

CHILDHOOD SEXUAL ABUSE (CSA) is one of the most traumatic and damaging experiences anyone can suffer. It can devastate the mind, body, and spirit. CSA influences and even forms the personality of its victims as well as their ability to protect themselves from further sexual violations.

As much as victims of childhood abuse try to forget what happened to them, the memory and the effects of the abuse can remain—robbing them of their self-confidence, their self-esteem and their sense of safety. Furthermore, the trauma can make it difficult for former victims to believe they deserve to be protected and respected and this sets them up for revictimization. This is because it creates great shame in its victims, causing them to feel worthless, dirty, unacceptable, and even unlovable.

Recovering from the trauma of childhood sexual abuse, although certainly possible, can be a long and arduous journey. And it can be a lonely one. Many former victims feel they have no one to reach out to for help, no one to tell their secret to, no one to validate their feelings and their experience. Those who can afford therapy and feel brave enough to reach out for help often don't know where to turn, and many hesitate because they don't know how to find a good therapist, one who is educated and experienced in trauma, one who is also caring and compassionate. *Thriving After Sexual Abuse* offers important information about how therapy works and suggests the right questions to ask potential therapists.

Whether you are in therapy or not, Denise will help you navigate this difficult journey. She opens her heart to her readers in order to not only share her own abuse experiences but to light the way for the travelers who come after her. She guides readers around obstacles on the path and lights the way to alternative paths that are safer and more likely to help former victims reach their destination.

Denise speaks directly to her readers, which is both engaging and soothing. Her compassionate voice throughout encourages readers to continue the process of healing even when it gets the toughest. She continues to reveal her own experiences throughout the book, sharing those practices, such as the benefits of exercise, yoga, meditation, and creative expression that were most beneficial to her. She moves on to offer strategies that can help readers deal with everything from how to handle triggers and body memories to who to tell and how to confront the perpetrator. She also addresses the controversial issue of forgiveness.

Denise ends the book by sharing her own inspirational poems—thus revealing still more of her own journey and modeling a way for readers to express their own feelings related to their recovery. The poems are both impactful and inspirational, offering readers a ray of hope in the midst of darkness.

I recommend this book to anyone who was sexually abused as a child or adolescent, whether you are female or male, whether you are currently in therapy or contemplating looking for a therapist. The book is particularly beneficial for those who are just beginning their healing journey as it offers nearly everything one needs to know about the process of recovery. This book is a gift to anyone healing from the devastation of childhood sexual abuse. Not only will it help you feel less alone, but her advice will steer you in the right direction, saving you not only time but unnecessary confusion and pain.

Introduction

MY NAME IS DENISE BOSSARTE, and I am a survivor of childhood sexual abuse. This book is my story of overcoming incest by my maternal grandfather.

In its pages, I share activities that aided my healing journey. I guide you to connect with healing practices. I help you work through tough questions and scenarios, such as deciding who to tell. And I help you understand what to expect on your journey to recovery.

I will first share my personal story of the sexual abuse I experienced at the hands of my grandfather. He was someone I should have been able to love and trust, but instead he used my love and trust against me. It is hard to write about what happened to me as a child and teenager. But I want you to know I understand what you went through and how you are suffering from the abuse still, long after it happened.

The remainder of the book is dedicated to detailing the activities of my healing journey. I share what I did and how it impacted my life and aided my healing. And I create a space for you to explore a healing journey for yourself and offer a list of selected resources you can review for additional help and information.

Please be aware the next section you are about to read contains a recounting of traumatic sexual abuse. You may prefer to skip to the next section on "How to Use This Book" if you have concerns about being triggered.

My Journey

I'm not sure how other people remember their childhoods, what details they can recall. But from the way people talk, they are connected to those past events and see them as part of themselves.

That's not how it is for me.

As a child, I learned to forget, to block out the memories that were too painful or frightening to remember. I learned early to lock memories behind closed doors in my mind. But that wasn't something that I was able to do selectively, so the good memories were trapped away with the bad.

To save myself, I set aside my childhood self and became a separate soul, one forced to quickly leave childhood behind. I pushed that little girl to the deep recesses of my mind, eventually forgetting she was even there. I forgot her, with her scabbed knees and frightened eyes. I only started to remember fragments in high school when my grandfather was in the hospital dying of prostate cancer. I never knew the whole story, the whole truth, but there was more than enough to remember him by.

It took me a long time to feel safe enough to remember things from my childhood because to remember the good meant the hurt and pain could also come out unexpectedly.

Can I say when every instance of abuse happened? Not really. I can only guess from the clues about how old I might have been.

My earliest memories of the abuse are from when I was very young; when adults still towered over me. I remember seeing a photo of me as a baby sleeping with my grandfather on the sofa, lying on his chest, that made me wonder if the abuse started even then. But the abuse itself remains stubbornly separate from the timeline of my daily "normal" life.

Because of this separateness of timelines, it is hard for me to know exactly when the abuse started. I know the abuse was happening during elementary school, and it finally ended when he died when I was a freshman in high school.

After the abuse, I remember hating my body and my lack of control as hormones raged during my teen years. Hating the changes that drew his eyes like flies to a corpse. Hating the shape that tempted him to dare touch what wasn't offered. I abhorred the sensations that carried such baggage, such memories of control and pain. I hated my futile efforts to thrust the abuse away as it clung stubbornly to my soul, encased me in a constant reminder of his touch. Until I dared to dream of using my hands to kill myself, end it all, and set myself free.

I grew to hate him. Fuck him, the bastard, for being so self-ish, for doing what he did. For being so smug, thinking he could get away with it, hide it, that no one would know or find out. I wanted him to suffer as I did, to be the instrument of his pain, all the while knowing this would make me just like him—a monster.

I wanted to hide from my memories of abuse and hide myself from the world. So I clothed myself in baggy sweatshirts and worn jeans, tearing down my self-esteem and building up self-loathing. All the while I hoped that Love would find me. I hoped to be seen through my clashing fear and yearning, for someone to push bravely past the walls I'd constructed, confident of my worthiness where I wasn't.

But the world was full of strangers, people far from me. Wary, I watched them living. What was it that everyone else seemed to know but me? How did they waltz through life so sure of themselves, of the steps? I constantly looked around me, searching for understanding, for happiness, for acceptance from those who surrounded me. I didn't feel any connection, just two left feet. I felt I was at the mercy and the judgment of people I despised for their enjoyment in a world where I was a stranger.

I was so angry! Angry at feeling out of control. Angry because I could not feel connected or loved. And I used my anger against myself. I created a rigid outer shell to contain the turmoil inside that raged and roiled and fought for release in tears and screams that were never released, remaining caged inside.

Eventually I feared happiness because I had learned repeatedly through my childhood of the inevitable pain that would follow, pain much greater in comparison. I was waiting for the other shoe to drop, waiting to have the universe yank away any possibility of joy when I least expected it. To me, the universe was not dispassionate or uncaring about my happiness. But it was joyfully, gleefully waiting for the exact moment when I was calm and confident and unwatchful, when it would be the most painful, then it would snatch the rug out from under my feet and leave me torn and bleeding. Eventually, I got to a place where I'd rather be numb and untouched than suffer the pain again.

I grew obsessed with school and strived for perfection. I pushed myself with physical exertion to the point of pain, ate less or nothing. Drove fast at night over hilly roads with the radio blasting, played cat and mouse with death and hoped to lose.

I was constantly doing, running from the responsibilities. Responsibilities to be good, to be kind, to give understanding and acceptance to all aspects of myself, regardless of their origin or their ugly faces. I grew tired. Tired of running from myself, like a rat in a cage, circling restlessly, endlessly on the wheel. Yet I couldn't slow down though the pace was killing me, killing my hope and my sanity, because the fear of failure, of failing myself, was too great.

A friend told me I would never completely "get over it" or "move on from it" until I could accept and forgive. But how could I forgive all the people who should have known and done something? How could I forgive him?

So instead, I decided to work on forgiving myself. To welcome back my wounded little girl self into my life and find ways that she and I could heal together.

Years later, I read a story of a man who could travel through time. He met a girl and became her guardian, protecting her from the harm he knew would find her. But he didn't protect her from all the pain because he knew it was the pain that made her strong and made her who and what she was.

I realized that was what the universe had given me: a chance to learn, to overcome. Looking back, in hindsight, I know I am the person I am, here and now, because of all that happened.

How to Use this Book

This book is for anyone who has survived sexual abuse and for partners of survivors. Although my personal experiences of sexual abuse may not mirror yours, I believe you will connect with the emotional, psychological, mental, and spiritual anguish I experienced and describe in this book.

I am not a mental health professional trying to sell you on a program of "Find Your Freedom in 21 Days" or "6 Steps to Reclaiming Your Life." I am a survivor with a PhD in developmental neuroscience, a contemplative arts teacher, trained meditation facilitator, and a published author with a novel based on my abuse experience.[1] My goal in writing this book is to share the practices I developed and the experiences I engaged in to help me overcome my sexual abuse and to *thrive* in a life I love.

This book is not a tell-all of my abuse, although writing it has served as a catharsis for me in my journey of healing that I began in college and continues today. With this goal in mind, I will share some information about my sexual abuse, but the bulk of this book will be about what happened afterward—the things I did to move on with my life and find joy and freedom.

I mean for this book to be an inspiration and a resource for your journey of healing. In each chapter, I will share my thoughts and experiences as they relate to the chapter topic. I include questions at the end of each chapter to encourage you to explore what you learned from my experiences and to plan how you can incorporate the lessons into your own journey of healing. I recommend getting a notebook or journal to write down your answers to the chapter questions. When I started my healing journey, I felt overwhelmed and lost not knowing where to go and what to do to get help. I wished at the time there were instructions to help me find what I needed—step-by-step instructions in fact. At the end of the chapters, I provide detailed information in the form of questions for you to journal on. There is no requirement for you to complete all

---

[1] My novel, *GLAMOROUS*, is available on Amazon.com: https://amzn.to/2Xsc16Q

the questions. These areas are guides to help you find what you need at your own pace. You can complete the questions immediately after reading the chapter, or return and work through them at your own pace as they serve you.

If you are just starting a healing journey, then I recommend reading the book from cover to cover in the order it is presented. If you have already started on your healing journey, then you may want to skip the chapters on Individual Therapy, Group Therapy, and Medication and jump to the chapter on Self-Help books.

Life doesn't come with guarantees. And getting back your sense of joy, freedom, and self is hard work—fucking hard work!

But I know that with the help of this book, you can overcome your abuse, become a Thriver, and live a life you love.

What to Expect

STARTING A HEALING JOURNEY can be a terrifying thing to contemplate. Even though you are living a life filled with feelings of despair, worthlessness, or anger, asking yourself to make a shift to change can be overwhelming to consider. Where you are now may be miserable, but it is a misery you know well. What might happen if you decide actively to pursue moving away from the pain-generating past to something else? Is it even possible?

In this book, I offer several practices and experiences to help you start and provide ongoing support for your healing journey. To deal with the fear of change and fear of failure, I suggest starting with two things: (1) finding a therapist for individual therapy, and (2) pick one healing practice you've read that resonated with you, one thing that you think you can do now and start it.

Take baby steps in starting your healing journey. Don't set yourself up for failure. Don't overcommit yourself beyond what you can realistically handle emotionally, mentally, and physically right now. Know that this is a healing journey, not a "fix yourself in a weekend" approach.

Be gentle with yourself as you start. Give yourself time to try something you think will aid and support you, time to see if it is right for you and moves you forward toward thriving. After a time, you may find that what you are trying is not working for you. Without beating yourself up, let go of what you were trying and see what else might work for you instead. This process is like planting seeds and then watering and fertilizing them over time to see the flowers grow and bloom. They won't all germinate, but with the proper attention, they—like you—can thrive.

A Healing Journey
A healing journey is about both letting go and welcoming. It's about letting go of thoughts, feelings, behaviors, and even people that are not serving you. It's about welcoming and incorporating thoughts, feelings, behaviors, and people that will empower, enrich, and energize your life.

One thing to expect as you work on yourself is that memories, emotions, and physical sensations related to the abuse will come up. You may have been spending a lot of energy, even subconsciously, trying to hold back the memories and the pain they cause. But from my personal experience, and knowledge gained from working with mental health professionals, avoiding dealing directly with the issues of the abuse won't keep them from permeating your life. Quite the opposite.

The abuse can start permeating every aspect of your life: your relationship with yourself, your relationship with other people, work, play, downtime—everything. Ignoring a festering wound doesn't heal it. It must be lanced and treated before it can no longer have an impact.

That is why I have stated that getting an individual therapist is a critical part of the process. You need someone to help you work through things as things come up. As you open one closed door after another, cleaning house and opening windows to let the air and light in, having someone there to help you go through all the "stuff," to help you know what to keep and what to throw out, is vital.

I encourage you to purchase a notebook or journal and record the information for each of the questions below there. You will be using this notebook or journal in subsequent chapters of this book to capture important information for your healing journey.

Things to Consider as You Start Your Healing Journey
- What are you looking to let go of on your healing journey?
- What thoughts about yourself do you want to change? What negative thoughts do you want to release?
- What parts of your life do you want to change? What negative actions and behaviors do you want to release?
- What are you looking to bring into your life on your healing journey?
- What positive thoughts about yourself do you want to embrace?
- What positive actions and behaviors do you want to embrace?
- What affirmations and aspirations can you make for yourself?
- Where can you display these affirmations and aspirations so you see them daily? Your mirror, your desk, your phone?

Part I: GETTING HELP

The first chapters of this book are around things I believe are foundation elements to work with on your healing journey: therapy, meditation, and self-help books. How you work with them will be a very personal process that will evolve.

CHAPTER 2

Individual Therapy

I BELIEVE ONE OF THE MOST IMPORTANT THINGS you can do to begin your journey of healing is to find a therapist who you can work with one-on-one.

Over the course of my healing journey, I worked with several therapists. Working with a therapist gave me a safe place to talk about what had happened to me without having to fear how the person listening to me would react.

I didn't have to spend my energy bracing to deal with someone who might deny what I said happened to me. I didn't have to worry about making sure the other person was okay so that what I told them would not drive them out of my life. I have never lost someone from my life by revealing, but I worried that it could happen.

I could focus on looking at what had happened to me. I could talk openly, without holding back, about how the abuse had impacted my life and how I felt about myself because of it.

With a therapist, I worked with someone trained to understand the power the experiences had over me, both in the past while they were happening to me as a child and still in the present as an adult. Someone wholly in my corner who had the skills to help me work through things. And someone who would not let me get away with any bullshit when I tried to avoid doing the work I needed to continue on my healing journey. The therapist helped me to keep a delicate balance between pushing myself and nurturing myself. She helped me to move through the effects the abuse was having on my life.

My First Therapy Experience

My first experience with therapy did not go very well. I was in elementary school when my personality shifted in response to the abuse by my grandfather. I went from a loving, vibrant, and outgoing child to one withdrawn and uncommunicative, one with nightmares and fear about going to my grandparents' house, although I don't remember talking with parents about my fears. My parents recognized the outward change but did not know what it meant.

There wasn't a lot of information out there about sexual abuse when I was a child, and few professionals specialized in dealing with sexual abuse, particularly in children. I think my parents did the best they could under the circumstance.

Unfortunately, the best they could do at the time was to take me to their marriage counselor. I remember feeling furious at having to go see their psychologist. I don't remember my parents explaining to me why they were taking me there. What I remember is feeling they thought something was wrong with me, and they wanted it fixed so I could go back to being their little girl again.

The psychologist tried to have a conversation with me about what was going on. But I was so pissed off I would not answer him. I sat there analyzing his office with the soft colors to soothe, the plush chair to make me comfortable, and the handy Kleenex in case I needed to cry, which I refused to do.

He ended up giving me a written psychological test designed for adults. Again, not much in the way of resources at that time, but I shake my head to think about it now.

The test asked questions like if I believed Jesus talked to me and was asking me to do things, if I heard voices, that type of thing. Several of the questions repeated throughout the test, and I remember getting even more upset, thinking, "How stupid do they think I am not to remember this question?" I knew they were looking to catch me giving a different answer each time it was asked. I can't remember if I stubbornly selected the same answer each time or if I played games by choosing different answers. As pissed as I remember being, it was probably the latter.

In the end, the psychologist told my parents I was a normal child going through a phase that I would get over soon. I guess my parents believed him because they never took me to another psychologist, and we went forward as if nothing had happened.

Looking back at that experience is painful. I cringe at how everything was handled, but those were the times then. I also deeply regret not sharing anything about what was going on with my grandfather and not getting help then when the abuse was occurring. It would be many years before I confided in anyone else, and even longer before anyone encouraged me to get help to deal with the abuse.

These days, I believe parents and other adults are more aware of the signs that a child is being abused, many of which I exhibited in elementary school.

I recently got a job with a school district and had to go through new employee training on recognizing the signs that a child is being sexually abused. As I sat there doing the self-paced online course, it triggered me into anxiety and anger as, one by one, I recognized the signs as ones I showed. And I was filled with anxiety from the memories evoked by that list of warning signs, and anger at my parents for not recognizing what was going on at the time.

Later Therapy Experiences

My next experience with therapy was much better. I was in college then and confided to a graduate student I was dating about the abuse. He encouraged me to go to the student counseling center to speak with someone about it.

I did not like the first counselor I met with. She seemed very uptight and was judgmental about the fact I was dating two people at the same time—one local and one long-distance. Rather than talking with me about what was best for me in the dating situation, I felt she was judging me from a moral high ground. I didn't go back to that therapist.

But I was determined to get help. Something inside of me pushed me to continue to reach out and try to find a professional to help me, and that something was stronger than any fear of sharing my story with a stranger.

I found another therapist from the student counseling center who I loved. She was very easy to connect with and very easy to talk to. I worked with her for a couple of years until I graduated from college. She helped me a great deal along my healing journey. She also connected me to group therapy and Survivors of Incest Anonymous (SIA), which I will describe in the next section of the book.

One thing to note was that although I was in therapy, I had still not confided in my parents about the abuse. To do the counseling, my parents needed to pay for it. So I told my parents I was under a lot of stress from school and wanted to talk with someone. Luckily that was enough for them to cover the cost.

My final work with a therapist came when I was a graduate student. My fiancé and I were engaged a few years prior during my first graduate degree but broke up. Now in my second graduate degree program and engaged to him again, I wanted to have a neutral person to talk to about my past and my planned future with my fiancé.

I was working and going to school and was able to find a therapist through my insurance plan.

She and I spent several months before the wedding and after working through my lingering issues from the abuse. We also worked on preparing me for marriage; how the relationship would challenge me and my abilities and perspectives with intimacy.

She was wonderful in having a very accurate bullshit detector. She helped me see where there was room for improvement in my relationship based on changing my behavior or my fiancé changing his. She even had him come to a session to work together. She and I worked together until it came to the point we were just socializing during our sessions, and I realized that my time with her was complete.

Although I had some not-so-helpful experiences with therapy in the beginning of my healing journey, I ended up finding the therapists I needed to move me through some very challenging times and get me to where I could live my life with freedom and joy.

> I found my therapist by calling my insurance company and asking for the names of female therapists who worked with survivors of childhood abuse.
>
> It was a terribly difficult phone call to make, to say that to a total stranger. But my desire for help overcame my fear of shame.
>
> You can find the therapists that is right for you in a number of ways.
>
> In the "Finding and Working with a Therapist" below, I list several options.

The work I did with the therapists was critical for me. Someone objective, someone who wanted me to heal was there for me.

She was someone who could give me a perspective beyond shame and blame and provide me tools for my healing journey.

Your Individual Therapy

I believe that working with a mental health professional will be one of the biggest factors in your healing journey. Feelings can resurface throughout your lifetime. Seeking counseling as you need it is a very self-loving and nurturing gift. I recommend that you work with someone who not the same gender (gender-identification) as the person who abused you to avoid being triggered.

I also recommend that you work alone with your therapist and do not include your partner, if you have one, until you and the therapist believe it would be of benefit.

Understanding Therapists and Their Credentials

"Therapist" is the umbrella term for professionals trained to provide treatments. Therapists can be marriage counselors, social workers, life coaches, psychoanalysts, psychologists, licensed professional counselors, and other master's- and doctoral-level mental health practitioners. These practitioners will focus on working with different types of patients in one or more "practice areas." These practice areas can include couples, families, children, grief, trauma/PTSD, depression, anxiety, sexual abuse/rape, and others.

Psychiatrists are trained medical doctors who may prescribe medications. The focus of their time with a patient may be the management of medication as a course of treatment. Often a psychologist and a psychiatrist will work together to coordinate the best therapy for a patient.

Practitioners may or may not be licensed. A practitioner becomes licensed when they have completed the educational and work experience required and have passed an exam for licensure. This ensures you are getting care by a qualified and experienced therapist.

The titles below are ones given to licensed professionals. Any of these professionals can help you on your healing journey.

- LPC—licensed professional counselor
- LMFT—licensed marriage and family therapist
- LMHC—licensed mental health counselor
- LCPC—licensed clinical professional counselor
- LCSW—licensed clinical social worker
- LMSW—licensed master social worker
- LISW—licensed independent social worker
- LICSW—licensed independent clinical social worker
- ANP—advanced nurse practitioner
- LPA—licensed psychological associate

Practitioners also exist who have earned master's and doctorate degrees.

- MS—master of science
- MA—master of arts
- MSW—master in social work
- PhD—doctor of philosophy, a psychologist
- PsyD—doctor of psychology

- MD—doctor of medicine

Regardless of their licensing or their degrees, the most important thing is to find a therapist you are comfortable with and who you feel can help you on your healing journey.

Finding and Working with a Therapist

Below I share recommended steps to take in finding a therapist. I encourage you to take the time to include the information for each of the steps into your notebook/journal.

1. **The first step is to research therapists. Below are suggestions for approaches to identify potential therapists.**

    ☐ If you have insurance, call your insurance company to find out how to locate a therapist who specializes in women's issues or sexual abuse/rape.

    - Write the number for your insurance company in your notebook/journal.

    When you speak with them, find out the following information. Make note of answers to the questions below in your notebook/journal.

    - How many sessions are covered each year?
    - Are there any restrictions, like in-network versus out-of-network providers?

- What is the amount that insurance would not cover, i.e. my out-of-pocket expense?
- Will the cost apply to your annual deductible and annual out-of-pocket maximum?
- Can you use a Flexible Spending Account (FSA) or Healthcare Spending Account (HSA) to cover the cost?

☐ Do a search online on your insurance provider's website to locate therapists who specialize in women's issues, sexual abuse, or rape.

- Write the insurance website address in your notebook/journal.

☐ Do some searching online to find therapists in your area who specialize in sexual abuse/rape.

☐ Use the online Psychologist Locator tool by the American Psychological Association: https://locator.apa.org/

☐ Use the online Find A Therapist tool at Psychology Today: https://www.psychologytoday.com/us/therapists

☐ Use the online Find the Right Therapist tool at GoodTherapy: https://www.goodtherapy.org/find-therapist.html

☐ Use the online tool with Open Path psychotherapy collective: https://openpathcollective.org/. The therapists provide affordable, in-office and online psychotherapy sessions.

☐ Explore the licensed therapists available virtually on the BetterHelp website https://www.betterhelp.com/ and TalkSpace website https://try.talkspace.com/.

☐ Explore other virtual therapy sites through healthline.com: https://www.healthline.com/health/our-top-10-online-therapy-picks.

☐ If you are in school, see what options are available through your student health center.

☐ Ask your physician or another health professional.

☐ Search for "therapist organizations" online to find groups with local representation in your area.

☐ Call the local or state psychological association. Write the associations' numbers in your notebook/journal.

☐ Contact an area community mental health center. Write the mental health center numbers in your notebook/journal.

☐ Inquire at your church, synagogue, temple, mosque, or house of worship.

☐ If you are comfortable doing so, check with your friends and network to see if they have recommendations for a therapist.

2. **The second step is to make a list of options for therapists.**

   For each therapist, write the following information in your notebook or journal:

   • Name
   • Address
   • Phone Number
   • Website
   • Type of license

3. **The third step is to call the therapists and ask questions.** The questions below are ones to consider asking before making an appointment. You might not need to ask all of

these questions if your research has provided the answers, but these are helpful for vetting the different therapists. Be sure to write the answers to these questions in your notebook/journal for each therapist.

- Do you offer a complimentary first session?
- How many years have you been practicing?

Share with the therapist that you are a survivor of sexual abuse. Write the answers to the following questions in your notebook/journal.

- What experience do you have helping people like me?
- What experience do you have working with survivors whose abuser was a family member?
- What special training have you had?
- What kinds of methods or techniques do you use in working with survivors? Why?
- Do you set goals with your clients? Why or why not? If so, how do you go about doing that?
- Is family reconciliation a goal? Why or why not?
- What do you believe is the outcome of sexual abuse therapy?
- Do you use group therapy?
- Do you incorporate other healing methods, like music, art, body work, or others? What kinds?
- What are your fees? Do you have a sliding-scale fee policy?
- How long are your sessions?

- Will you accept direct billing to or payment from my insurance company?
- Are you affiliated with any managed care organizations?
- Do you accept Medicare or Medicaid insurance?
- Are you available for emergency phone calls and appointments?

4. **The fourth step is to schedule an appointment with your first choice of therapist.** Be sure to mark the date and time in your calendar.

5. **The fifth step is to be sure to keep the appointment!**

   It may take pushing through your fear to do this, but you can do it!

If you are struggling with anxiety about your upcoming appointment, it can help to write down all the reasons why you made the appointment.

You can make a list for all the things you hope to release from your life through therapy. And you can also make a list of all the things you hope to invite into your life through therapy.

Revisit these lists any time you feel anxiety about your appointment surfacing.

6. **The sixth step is to evaluate your first visit.**

    The biggest part of your work with the therapist will be based on the relationship you have with them. Just as critical as your commitment to healing will be your relationship with the therapist.

    Be honest with yourself—do you feel safe with this person, and can you work with them?

    You will do difficult work under this person's care. Make sure you are comfortable with how this person is treating you and addressing your issues.

    Understand that re-exposure to the past trauma is not necessary. With over 500 approaches to therapy, you will have options for working with a therapist and an approach that works for you. You can read more about the different types of therapy styles at https://www.betterhelp.com/advice/counseling/the-different-types-of-counseling-styles.

    You have the right to set boundaries in your sessions, and to understand why the therapist is asking you certain questions or asking you to do particular things. This is your therapy, and you need to be an active participant in what goes on in your sessions.

    Don't stop seeing a therapist just because the work is hard, but if it doesn't feel right, move on to the next person on your list.

7. **The seventh step is to commit to seeing the therapist as often as you can.**

   If you have insurance, take advantage of the number of sessions you have available through your plan. Weekly sessions are usually a good place to start, but you and your therapist will decide what is best for your circumstances. Too much time between sessions and you might feel like you are starting from scratch. Make adjustments to your schedule so that you can commit to the time you need to work with your therapist.

   Know that building a trusting relationship with a therapist takes time.

   The more time you commit to working with a therapist, the more you will support your healing journey.

Group Therapy

ANOTHER IMPORTANT ASPECT OF HEALING is connecting to a group of people who have experienced sexual abuse at some point in their lives.

While I was going through therapy in college, my therapist recommended that I join a therapy group for people dealing with sexual abuse. She connected me with two groups: a small women's group run by another local therapist, and a SIA group for men and women.

> The idea of joining a group may be intimidating to you. Your first reaction may be "I don't want to share something so private with strangers."
>
> You can have tremendous benefits by sharing your story and experiences with other people who have gone through similar experiences.

Knowing that you are not alone and that others are there to support you can have a tremendous impact on your healing.

I share below how powerful and positive the group experiences were for me.

Small Women's Group

The women's group had three members when I joined. They included: a woman raped when she delivered a pizza, a woman whose uncle had molested her as a child, and a woman who had suffered sexual abuse by members of her family. The three members of the group varied in occupations and in age were from their early twenties to middle age.

At first, the therapist did not want to include me in the group because I was in my senior year of college and would not be with the group long before I graduated. She did not want to disrupt the group or have them impacted by my leaving so quickly compared to the time the others had and would be in the group. Eventually, she relented and let me into the group. In the end, she told me that she was happy I joined, as I brought a unique voice to the healing process for the members.

For the first time I was opening up to total strangers, not my therapist or a boyfriend. It was very scary to share my story, but the women in the group were very supportive of me. When I heard their stories, I realized why they could be so understanding: they had gone through things as traumatic as me or things I thought worse than I'd experienced.

Our group met weekly, and I learned so much as these women shared what they were going through and how they were trying to heal their lives. Their success and their setbacks, their tears and their joy were ones I recognized in my life, despite our differences in age and occupation.

The woman whose uncle had molested her had been working on her healing journey for several years. I saw in her a role model for how I might move beyond my post-traumatic thinking and responses to a place of healthy living and choices. She eventually left the group because she and the therapist decided it was time for her to move on from the support of the group. I remember being extremely jealous of her being so healthy, but at the same time, I was determined to find my way to where she was in my own healing journey.

Survivors of Incest (SIA) Group

Soon after I started attending the all-women's group, I joined an SIA group. I was dating a graduate student who attended Alcoholics Anonymous (AA) meetings, and he helped me find an SIA meeting at a local church. It was a closed meeting, meaning only survivors could attend, so my boyfriend could not go with me.

My boyfriend shared how AA meetings went and I figured SIA would be similar in structure. But it still terrified me to go to the meeting. It was nearly impossible for me to do anything radically outside my normal safe and controlled routine. But individual therapy was helping, and group therapy was making a difference, so I told myself it was worth the fear and anxiety to attend.

When I walked in for the first time, I nearly turned around and left. There were at least a dozen people there, and there were men there, too. Somehow it didn't occur to me that there would be men there! I guess I had a mental block about that because of my abuser being male, and I couldn't imagine men being victims, only aggressors.

But my stubborn side kicked in, and I sat down to see what would happen. They read from a pamphlet as the official guide for SIA meetings. The thing that struck me was the definition of incest:

> We define incest very broadly as a sexual encounter by a family member, or by an extended family member, that damaged the child. By "extended family" member we mean a person that you and/or your family have known over a period of time. This may be any family member, a family friend, clergy, another child, **or anyone who betrayed the child's innocence and trust.** We believe we were affected by the abuse **whether it occurred once or many times** since the damage was incurred immediately. By "abuse" we mean any sexual behavior or contact with the child. Sexual contacts may include a variety of verbal and/or physical behaviors; penetration is not necessary for the experience to be defined as incest or sexual abuse.[2]
>
> *Note: Emphasis is mine.*

The definition of a family member seemed so broad to me. I was definitely an easily defined incest survivor because my

---

[2] https://siawso.org/about/

abuser was my biological grandfather. But I was not aware that the definition of abuser moved beyond the immediate family. That meant there could be many people out there like me who considered themselves victims of incest.

I also was relieved to hear them read that it was okay for me to be there "whether it had occurred once or many times." I only had a few memories of the times my grandfather had molested me, and I questioned whether I could call myself a victim if it happened "so few times." Obviously, I was not thinking straight, as I oscillated between feeling to blame for what had happened and also feeling like I should deny it since it only happened a few times that I could recall.

As we went around the room and people shared about their experiences, I started to realize that everyone there was dealing with pain and suffering like me.

There was a woman struggling in her marriage to feel safe and comfortable having sex with her husband. She ended up getting a yeast infection each time they did have sex.

There was a red-headed young man, not much older than me, who was a model. He talked about being abused by the truck drivers at his father's truck stop, and how his father was so disengaged from raising the kids that he let that happen. He described how he went to summer camp, and when he got a letter from his father, it was addressed to his twin who was still at home. He also talked about traveling and how he got picked up hitchhiking by a couple who forced him to have sex with them. His story really impacted me. At the time, I felt ugly and unlovable yet here was someone I envied for being gorgeous who was suffering in the same ways I was.

The person who affected me the most at that first meeting was an older man. I am not sure how old he was, but he had gray-hair and reminded me of my grandfather a bit because of his age. When he spoke, he broke down while describing how his mother had sexually abused him as a child. I could not believe a person I was mentally putting in the same corner of my mind as my grandfather had suffered as I did. And to suffer so long—to still be struggling at his age.

It was a lot to take in at my first meeting, but I knew from what they shared that this was a place where I could be with people who understood me. It took me quite a while to get up the courage to share my story, but I met nothing but support and understanding when I did.

I learned in attending the meetings how people were and were not doing the work they needed to move forward on a healing journey. I did not want to be like the people who seemed to never get past what had happened to them and kept reliving things. I wanted to be like the ones who were struggling but were also making changes to their lives that were taking them away from the trauma of the abuse into a new life. They were great teachers, and I am so thankful I found that group while still in school.

Joining a Group

Think about the group you would like to join. When starting any kind of group, it can be helpful to commit to going to a series of sessions (three to six) as it can take time to feel comfortable. That being said, if there is something about the group you cannot tolerate (such as a group that allows smoking and you're a nonsmoker), look for a different group.

Each group will develop its own dynamics based on the people in the group and the culture the group members have created for themselves. You have a right to set boundaries in the group just as you do in individual therapy. If you feel the group is not providing the support you need to continue on your healing journey, especially if the group is encouraging unhealthy coping strategies or leading you to create new ones, it is time to consider moving to a new group. Always be willing to do self-evaluation on whether the work you are doing is moving you toward healing or holding you back.

A good online resource for finding a group is the website for the American Group Psychotherapy Association (AGPA) https://www.agpa.org/ where you can search for a certified group therapist. Other online resources for finding groups are provided in the Resources section at the end of the book.

What Type of Group is Right For You?

Write the answers to the follow questions in your notebook/journal.

- What kind of group are you interested in joining? One led by a mental health professional, a group like SIA, or a group run by other survivors?
- Do you want to join a group that is mixed gender, or do you want a group that is only your gender?

You might feel more comfortable with a group that is the same gender if your abuser was of a different gender.

But also consider how healing it might be to hear survivor stories from people of the opposite gender, even the gender of your abuser.

Attending a mixed gender group facilitated some of the most powerful healing on my journey.

- Do you want to join a group that is only survivors, or one that includes partners of survivors?

Being a part of a group that includes only survivors can allow a greater sense of safety and freedom to share your story, especially to a level of detail you might not be comfortable with in a partner-inclusive group.

But with a partner-inclusive group, there is an opportunity for you (and possibly your partner) to learn and grow from the viewpoints and experiences of partners of survivors.

Finding Groups for Survivors of Sexual Abuse

You can reuse the Finding a Therapist checklist from Chapter 2 to find local survivor groups meeting in your area. Write the answers to the checklist in your notebook/journal.

Several organizations have meetings for survivors. Some of these groups offer in-person meetings, some offer phone meetings, and others offer online meetings and forums.

Besides directories for finding local groups, these organizations provide other resources such as monthly newsletters, online and downloadable materials, manuals, books, and links to useful resources, to name a few. Several of these organizations also have a social media presence. It is worth visiting these organizations' websites to explore what resources and materials are available from each one.

I provide a list of organizations and links to their websites in the Resources section at the end of the book. The links are provided as a convenience; including a link on this list does not imply endorsement.

CHAPTER 4

Medication

FROM THE EARLIEST POINT of remembering my abuse, it was important to me to rely on myself. I did not want to have to rely on something like medication. My mindset and stubbornness early on came from a combination of several things.

For one, I saw myself as broken, bad, damaged, and undeserving of love. Hadn't my parents dragged me to someone to try to "fix me?" Taking medication seemed like I'd be admitting that I *was* all these things. Admitting that I lacked the strength to make it without some external help. Admitting that I could not be in control of what happened to me, my body, or my mind.

The second reason I avoided medication was that I saw members of my family struggle through anxiety and depression. I saw how they worked with one medication after another to treat these mental health issues. Some of my family were more successful than others, but it seemed to me more often than not that things did not improve for them. That was the way it was with the medications that were available when I first started my healing journey in college. The third reason I avoided medication was that I strongly identified with being a smart person and excelling in academics. I feared that if I started on medication, it would impact my ability to be successful in academics and could impact my athletic ability, and I would lose a big part of my self-identity.

Symptoms of My Abuse

I experienced many symptoms common to survivors of sexual abuse during my childhood and into adulthood. These included: body image issues, nightmares, flashbacks, dissociation, anxiety, hypervigilance, eating issues, and suicidal thoughts. Although I was often sad or "down," at the time I never thought of myself as "depressed" because I could get out of bed each new day and function in my life in a way that seemed as normal as I could imagine.

I always felt different from other kids. Even before I understood what had happened to me, I felt bad, dirty, and unlovable. I felt no one would like me if they knew the real me.

I was also the smart and athletic kid growing up. That put me on the outside. It was hard to compare myself mentally and physically to my peers. And also hard for me to figure out how to compare myself to other kids my age to understand how they felt and lived emotionally.

Dealing with the Effects of My Abuse

Although things could get overwhelming for me, I found ways to "deal" with my situation. In elementary school, middle school, and high school, these included sports, music, and scholastics. I committed myself to activities and challenges that kept my body-focus on being an athlete, rather than being a vulnerable female, and my mind-focus on getting good grades.

I was on the girls' basketball team in middle school and high school. It was a mixture of being on the outside for being a female athlete, but also on the inside as a member of a team.

I was in the school band in elementary school and middle school, and in the marching and concert bands, with some moonlighting in the orchestra, in high school. I wanted to play the flute when I first started in band, but my mother always loved the French horn and convinced me to take up that instrument. I was usually one of only a few girls in the brass section—often the only one—and it was a lot more fun than if I'd been a part of the woodwinds where most of the other girls were. Everyone remembers the "band geeks," so once again I was on the outside in some ways at school but on the inside for being a part of the band.

I took as many AP/Honors classes as were offered in high school. I spent hours each night and every weekend doing homework to try to meet the high standards of these courses. I used studying as an excuse to avoid connecting more often with my peers and to keep my mind too busy to think about other things.

My self-identity hinged a great deal on my academic success. It was one of the things that made me feel like a "good" person, something that garnered recognition and reward rather than something I felt I needed to hide.

Finally, in college, I started therapy and working my own healing path as described in this book.

My Thoughts about Medication Today

I have several friends these days who take medication for depression. They've shared with me what it is like without the medication; they cannot live their lives without the help the medication provides them. They've shared how they wouldn't be able to get out of bed each morning, how they could not function throughout the day, or be able to be happy or joyful.

The medication gives them a chance at living a life they enjoy rather than dread. Most of them say they know that they will probably be on some form of medication for the rest of their lives, but it is worth it to them.

I have looked back and reconsidered whether my stubbornness served me well. Is it possible I could have had a more joyful life being on medication for my trauma symptoms? Or was the path I followed the best one for me?

I think I did what was right for me. I was never at a point where I felt I couldn't live my life in the way my friends described. And the trauma symptoms were never so overwhelming that I felt medication would be a resource I needed to engage.

For a long time, mine was a life of suffering. But I found a way to travel my own healing journey that did not include medication. I now appreciate, though, how critical it can be to get the right help for dealing with the symptoms of sexual abuse, particularly medication.

My advice to you is to work with your therapist to determine whether medication and psychiatric treatment can help you on your healing journey. It can be helpful to look at medication as a tool. But the work is still there to be done whether you have a tool or not.

Don't be like my stubborn younger self and discount the possibility that you could get an improved life through the use of medication. It won't be the magic bullet that makes your life what you want; there is still a lot of other work needed to heal from the sexual abuse. But you shouldn't ignore what could help you make the path to healing an easier one. Rely on the input and advice from mental health professionals who know your specific situation to guide your decision on the use of medication.

Seeking Psychiatric Help

Survivors can be impacted by sleep disturbances, anxiety, panic attacks, depression, suicidal thoughts, and other challenges that might not respond to counseling and therapy alone.

Psychiatric care that includes medication as a course of treatment could complement your therapy. This treatment is under the management of a psychiatrist who is a trained medical doctor who may prescribe medications based on a diagnosis. They will educate you on the benefits and risks of medications they think appropriate for the diagnosis and your situation.

Follow up with the psychiatrist about your experience with the medication, including any side effects. Our bodies are unique, and it can take some time to find the medication that's right for you.

Finding and Working with a Psychiatrist

Your therapist can advise you on connecting with a psychiatrist. You can also use the checklist in Chapter 2 to find a psychiatrist, and refer to Chapter 2 for questions to consider asking before you make an appointment. Write the answers to the questions in your notebook/journal.

Also keep in mind the two questions below, and include them as well:

- How much experience do you have in treating the trauma symptoms of sexual abuse, like (depression, anxiety, or your symptoms)?
- Are you willing to work with my other providers?

You can consider asking the following questions of the psychiatrist once you begin work with them. Write the answers in you notebook/journal.

- What is my diagnosis? How did you arrive at it? Please explain it in simple language that I can understand.
- What is the treatment plan you recommend?
- How did you pick the medication(s) for me?
- How well does the medication treat my symptoms?
- What can happen when I take the medication? What are the potential side effects?
- Am I likely to experience the side effects? Why?
- What are the potential risks of the medication?
- Are there medications you have considered that work better or have fewer side effects?
- Will the medication interact with my other prescriptions? With over-the-count products? With alcohol or caffeine?
- What should I do if the medication makes me feel worse?

Questions informed by "10 Questions to Ask a Psychiatrist or Therapist" from *Biopolar Disorder for Dummies* by Candida Fink and Joe Kraynak, 2005, Wiley Publishing, Inc., Hoboken, NJ.

Self-Help Books

ONE OF THE BEST PRACTICES I found in my healing journey was reading or listening to self-help books. I built up my own "Healing Works" library of books I felt could help me on my healing journey. I am still adding books to my library as I am constantly looking for ways to stretch myself and give myself more opportunities for healing. I take what works for me from the books and leave the rest. I found I enjoy having the paperback version of the books for taking notes, but ebook or audio versions of a Healing Works library might work better for you.

A note of caution about reading self-help books.

There is often content, particularly stories shared by survivors, that can be triggers of painful memories for survivors.

It is helpful to have a working relationship with a therapist and/or psychiatrist to help you deal with these
memories and the feelings they evoke.

The Book that Jumpstarted My Healing Journey

Early in my healing journey, I stumbled upon the book, *"The
Courage to Heal: A Guide for Women Survivors of Sexual Abuse,"* by
Ellen Bass and Laura Davis, which is I consider the definitive
guide for healing from sexual abuse. Finding this book shocked
me because I didn't know other women had gone through the
same experiences as children.

My healing journey started years before the #MeToo movement, and I felt all alone in my experiences. After years of feeling
isolated and by myself, here were stories from other survivors
bravely sharing their pain and their healing journeys. For the
first time, I felt myself hope that I could make it beyond my pain
and suffering to something better.

The Courage to Heal is much more than a set of survivor stories.
It includes explanations, strategies, and many resources for
body and emotional healing. The book is now in its fourth, twen-
tieth-anniversary edition and is available on Kindle, in
hardcover and paperback, and in audiobook format. I can't recommend this book more highly for the solid foundation it gave
me to begin my healing journey.

The authors have several related books, written together and
separately, that are worth adding to your Healing Works collec-
tion. I provide a list of their books in the Resources section at the
end of the book.

Harriet Lerner's books

Later in my healing journey, when I tried to learn how to be healthy in relationships and to be in healthy relationships, I found help in two books by Harriet Lerner, PhD (see the Resources section for titles).

There were two reasons for adding Harriet's books to my Healing Works library. First, while on my healing journey, I experienced a great deal of anger: anger at my abuser, anger at my family, anger at teachers, anger at anyone I thought should have figured out the abuse was happening and should have stepped in to stop it.

I was also angry with myself for "letting" the abuse happen and not stopping it. Looking back, I am sad at how long it took me to understand I wasn't to blame for what happened to me. It took me a long time to understand it intellectually, and even longer to accept it emotionally. I wanted to find compassion for my younger self who survived as best she could.

I was often striking out emotionally from this angry place at people in my life, but most of the time I turned that anger on myself because I did not know how to transform it into something else. I felt so bad about myself; the anger was another way to beat myself up for being a bad person.

The second reason I bought these books was that I wanted to have help in finding and living in a healthy relationship. Being abused screwed up what I understood about relationships. I didn't have great role models of healthy relationships in my family or in my friends' families. And although I had only been in a few romantic relationships up to that point in my life, I was tired of being in ones where I felt worse about myself rather than better.

These books gave me a way to work through my anger and find guidance on specific things to change to improve my self-image, to connect, and be healthier in relationships.

Brené Brown's books

In the past few years, I have discovered Dr. Brené Brown and her research on shame, vulnerability, and courage. I have read and listened to her books in audio format. Although her work does not specifically focus on abuse survivors, her research touches on many aspects of the feelings and emotional experiences of survivors.

Although she is a researcher, Brené writes in a style that's easy to understand and relate to for regular people. Her books are insightful and inspiring, bringing in the wisdom she has gleaned from her research. She also shares her personal stories: her struggles of being her not-so-best self, and working hard to live her life more authentically and fully.

I recommend reading Brené's books in the order of their publication, as her work grows and informs itself over time. I list her books in the Resources section at the end of the book from earliest to latest publication date.

I particularly enjoyed listening to *Braving the Wilderness* as an audible book because Brené read the audiobook herself!

HeatherAsh Amara's books

A set of books I have recently added to my Healing Works library are by HeatherAsh Amara; see Resources section.

HeatherAsh's books aren't focused on abuse survivors but are books to help women move beyond the limitations and expectations they have placed on themselves to live authentic and empowered lives. Her books provide rituals, exercises, and her own personal stories to guide the reader to a richer way of living.

HeatherAsh also offers several Warrior Goddess programs and has several Facebook sites to join other women in Warrior Goddess online communities.

I found her books to be helpful in challenging me to reconsider my habitual ways of thinking and living in the world. They were helpful for me to understand and integrate two aspects I struggled with throughout my life: the strong Warrior and the intuitive Goddess. Her works were the first place I saw where both energies/archetypes were considered as energies that one person could embody.

I've always been strongly tapped into my Warrior side, partly because I felt I needed to protect myself by being strong and partly because it was my personality to be focused, determined, and dedicated to my education, my career, and my projects. I was in touch, occasionally, with my Goddess side's unconditional love and wisdom, but felt that I would have to give up my Warrior side to live in my Goddess. HeatherAsh Amara's books helped me realize I could be both, and in doing so, I could be fully myself.

Beverly Engel's book

I recently discovered *It Wasn't Your Fault: Freeing Yourself from the Shame of Childhood Abuse with the Power of Self-Compassion* by Beverly Engel, LMFT. Beverly is a therapist and survivor of neglect and sexual, emotional, and physical abuse. Her book describes how debilitating shame is for survivors. She guides a reader to work through and get beyond the shame, culminating in her five-step Compassion Cure Program of self-understanding, self-forgiveness, self-acceptance, self-kindness, and self-encouragement.

I was deeply moved by Beverly's understanding of how shame dominates the world of survivors. It was often difficult for me to read about shame, as it resonated so deeply with me and brought up a lot of things related to my abuse. But her insights and her approaches on how to develop self-compassion to heal the shame are very powerful. Definitely a must-add to your Healing Library!

Rachael Denhollander and Kyla Harrison's books

I also recommend two memoirs for your Healing Works library: *What Is a Girl Worth: My Story of Breaking the Silence and Exposing the Truth about Larry Nassar and USA Gymnastics* by Rachael Denhollander, an attorney, advocate, and educator who was the first woman to speak out against former USA Gymnastics team doctor Larry Nassar, and *Fighting Back: What an Olympic Champion's Story Can Teach Us about Recognizing and Preventing Child Sexual Abuse—and Helping Kids Recover* by Kyla Harrison, two-time Olympic gold medalist in judo, and two mental health professionals, Cynthia S. Kaplan, PhD, and Blaise Aguirre, MD.

In *What is a Girl Worth*, Rachael describes her experiences as a gymnast and her abuse during medical treatments by Larry Nassar. Her book chronicles the impact the abuse had on her life and details the process of how she reported Larry Nassar and worked with other survivors to ensure Larry was prosecuted for his crimes against hundreds of women and girls. Seeing

Rachael's strength and determination to see justice done for the victims is such an inspiring read. And a hard awakening to the roadblocks and resistance that are integrated into our culture and justice system that hamper or even prevent abusers from being held accountable for their crimes.

In *Fighting Back*, Drs. Kaplan and Aguirre detail how Kyla's judo coach groomed her to be a victim of his sexual abuse and how the abuse devastated her life. The book combines excerpts from the journals Kayla kept throughout her childhood and teenage years with science-based information. It is meant to be a guide for parents and professionals to understand how abuse can happen, the signs of abuse, and how they can intervene and support victims' healing. I found it very helpful to see from the outside perspective how abuse can happen and continue, and the psychological and emotional factors that come in play for a victim during the abuse and after. It really brought home for me how I wasn't at fault and validated my experiences during and after the abuse.

The newest additions to my Healing Works library are books on cultivating resilience. I've learned that sexual abuse is a form of trauma, and have come to realize through my reading that a big step toward healing from trauma is building resilience. I realize now that the exercises and practices I share in this book are all ones that have gone toward building my resilience in a way that supports my healing.

> "Resilience is a well of inner resources that allows you to weather the difficulties and challenges your encounter without unnecessary mental, emotional or physical distress."
> *Everyday Resilience* by Gail Gazelle, MD

The books on resilience I have connected with are included in the Resources section at the end of the book. These books provide practical information and exercises that you can engage in to build your resilience. The authors are experienced therapists who are also long-time meditation practitioners: Gail Gazelle, MD, Rick Hanson, PhD, and Linda Graham, MFT. They bring their understanding of mindfulness and knowledge of neurobiology to their books and the recommendations they make.

Creating Your Own Healing Works Library

I suggest asking your therapist if they have recommendations for books that might be helpful for your specific situation.

Also, search Amazon.com for books related to sexual abuse and healing. You can also check out your local library for helpful books. Most libraries have an interlibrary loan system and also loan digital books you can read on your computer or other devices.

Not every book you find on sexual abuse and healing will be one that speaks to you or helps you on your healing journey. Use your best judgment about the content of the books for what makes sense to you and what you think you can add to your healing journey. You might return to a book many times during your journey to apply new things helpful for you at that specific point in your healing. Listen and trust your internal wisdom that is developing during your healing journey to guide you on what you need and what works for you.

Creating Affirmation Cards

A helpful thing I found while reading books from my Healing Works library was writing down quotes from the books that really struck me. I put them on my mirror so I could see and read them each morning as I got ready for work.

You can put them on your mirror, on your cell phone, as screensavers for your computer or phone, wherever you will see and be reminded of the positive and uplifting thoughts as frequently as possible.

Finding Your Inspiration

Spend some time with the questions below and write the answers in your notebook/journal.

- What books do you have on hand that can become the start of your Healing Works library?
- What passages in these books really speak to you?
- Are there more books by these authors that you could consider?
- Where could you place these quotes so you see them every day and they inspire you?
- What other books could you add to your Healing Works library?

- What books have friends or family recommended? Have any been referred to in other books you have read? Or shown up as "Also Bought" on Amazon.com?
- Are there any social media memes that really speak to you that you could tag, bookmark, save/screen capture?
- Which sources would you like to follow to have access to these inspirations regularly?

Part II: EMBRACING JOY

The next part of the book will focus on the practices and experiences I found that supported me in my growth from a Victim of incest to a Survivor of incest to a Thriver in the world.

DENISE BOSSARTE

CHAPTER 6

What Brings You Joy?

FINDING OUT WHAT BRINGS YOU JOY is a tremendous part of your healing journey. As a victim of incest, I bought into the belief I was damaged goods, that I didn't deserve love, and that I merited nothing good in my life. As a broken, unwanted thing, I deserved less than anyone else.

Some part of me, deep down inside, knew that was bullshit and fought in whatever way it could to keep me alive and reaching for joy and love in my life. Often it was unsuccessful, and my life seemed to be one of misery, pain, and loneliness. But some spark kept fighting and driving me toward my path of healing and the opportunities to bring and hold joy in my life.

Over the years I learned that working with my body and mind brings me joy. Doing yoga and other bodywork, going to the gym, walking, or biking all get me into my body and out of my head.

Being creative and exploring art is very healing. Whether it's grabbing my camera and heading outside for a bit of shooting, or trying my hand painting, gel printing, or knitting, or visiting museums, connecting with creativity brings me joy.

Being outside, experiencing the wonder of the natural world, playing with spontaneous nature mandalas, or soaking up the sights, sounds, and smells of a beautiful place brings me joy.

Simple things, like watching a good movie, reading a good book, or snuggling with the cat for an afternoon nap, bring me joy.

In his *New York Times* bestseller, *The Body Keeps the Score*, Dr. Bessel van Der Kolk discusses the large body of evidence that activities beyond traditional talk therapy can have an enormous therapeutic impact for survivors of trauma.

These activities include meditation, journaling, art, music, dance, theater, somatic body therapy, yoga, qigong, and other body work.

I try to challenge myself every few years to stretch and explore something different from my normal routine, something that will challenge me but also open me up to new possibilities. It's scary to push myself this way, but it has brought new experiences and practices that give me joy because of my willingness to step outside my comfort zone if only to try something once.

Finding Your Joy

Before continuing into the next chapters, take some time to reflect on the joy in your life. Write your answers to the questions in your notebook/journal.

- What is in your life that brings you joy?
- If it is being by yourself and doing things for yourself, what are those things?
- If it is being with and doing things with / for your family, what are those things?
- If it is being with and doing things with / for your friends, what are those things?
- If it is being with and doing things with /for your partner, what are those things?
- If it is being with and doing things with / for your pet(s), what are those things?

DENISE BOSSARTE

Physical Exercise

I FOUND IT VERY IMPORTANT to engage in physical activity when working along my healing journey.

I had become very disassociated from my body and became somewhat agoraphobic because of fear of both how I looked to other people based on how I felt about my body, and being afraid of other people who I saw as a threat to my safety.

But getting out and getting physical exercise was a way for me to reconnect to my body and also improve my self-image because I knew what I was doing was healthy for my body and would get my body into shape. I was doing something positive for my body rather than continuing to blame my body for the abuse or neglecting my body as a form of self-punishment.

What types of exercise can you enjoy during your healing journey?

You can do many activities by yourself, such as walking. But you can also connect with an exercise buddy, join a group (such as through Meetup.com), or take classes (through the gym, YMCA, or a community center) that would encourage you to get out and explore ways to connect with your body and get your body healthy.

What is important is that you find something that works for you!

Sports in College and Graduate School

Although I played basketball in high school, I didn't participate in any sports in college. One reason was that I was so focused on academics and getting good grades. The other reason was because I was too shy and embarrassed about my body to go to the gym or do any intramural activities. I ended up gaining thirty pounds my freshman year and being in the worst shape of my life, which did not help my issues with my self-image. I consoled myself that I excelled from a mental perspective and pushed aside any work on my body or my healing until later in college when I was ready to commit to working on my body and healing.

When I went to graduate school in biology in Boulder, Colorado, I entered with a large class of students. We were interested in doing things as a group and tried our hand at as many intramural sports as we could. We played flag football, basketball, volleyball, softball, and inner tube water polo. It was a great way to stay connected with my body while also joining in the comradery of team sports.

No one focused on how I looked or how my body looked. We were all out there trying our best and having fun. We were not stars individually, but we had many winning seasons throughout our graduate careers.

Because I'd been active in playing basketball in high school, I also played pickup basketball with graduate students, post-doctoral fellows, and professors. I was the only female on the court, but they treated me as one of the guys.

Being treated as a player rather than a female was wonderful. When we played, my body was not attracting unwanted attention from men—which amounted to just about ANY attention, unfortunately. On the court, they appreciated me for my athletic skill, not whether my physical appearance matched the expected norms of "beautiful" or "pretty" or "attractive." I could ignore the constant background thoughts about how I compared with other women. I could be me, playing the game.

While in graduate school, I also joined the Ultimate Frisbee co-ed city league and the Women's Club sports team. In the co-ed city league, I was one of many skilled women players who were appreciated for their physical skills playing the game. There was no sense of competition outside of being the best players we could be.

The Women's Club sports team provided a real healing experience for me. Luckily I got to play on a team of mostly graduate students from all different departments on campus. Here were true role models of women who excelled academically in challenging fields such as biology, biochemistry, ecology, and psychology, and being awesome athletes. We traveled several times during our season, and our team was successful enough to make it to the national competition and place fourth.

I'd always felt so different from other girls and women growing up. I felt tainted and that I could never compare with the girls or women in school and out in the world because of my horrible self-image. I felt unlovable and un-want-able and always felt a sense of isolation and being an outsider.

All the experiences in graduate school helped me start reconnecting with my body and let me see that I was as capable as these other women. That I could bond with other women like I never felt I could before. I still had my hang-ups at the time for my emotional and spiritual well-being, but at least I started to find a way to appreciate my body rather than loathe it.

Physical Activity For Me Today

Since getting out of school, I have tried several different physical activities for exercise and fun. I have done a lot of walking and biking, with some rollerblading, water and snow skiing, and hiking. I have had knee issues since high school, so walking, rather than running, works best for me. And the walking gets me out into nature, which I love and find especially healing. See Chapter 9 *Being Out in Nature*.

Now, besides walking outside as much as I can (with or without my camera), I go to the gym to work on my physical strength and stamina. I am lucky my husband also goes to the gym and is very experienced with weight lifting and aerobic exercise, so he helps me put together a program that works for me. Arm strength is important as I age, and I like to have the strength to support my other healing practices, such as yoga. I also look to increase and then maintain my physical stamina so my husband and I can enjoy our bike rides during the warmer weather.

Before starting any new physical activity, it is always good to discuss your plans with your primary care doctor.

Some Things for You to Try

When choosing activities, consider where can you find or engage in these activities near you, and when you can do these activities within your schedule.

This list is just a start. What other activities can you add? Write your answers in your notebook/journal.

- walking
- running
- biking
- hiking / climbing
- ice skating
- roller blading / skating
- water skiing
- snow skiing / snowboarding
- swimming (lap swimming, water polo, synchronized swimming, diving)
- water aerobics
- tennis
- racquetball
- dancing (ballroom, salsa, country, pole)
- horseback riding
- canoeing/kayaking /rafting
- team sports (soccer, volleyball, basketball, badminton, softball, bowling, and other sports)
- working out at the gym

- weightlifting
- hula hooping, jumping rope
- your favorite activity

Yoga and Other Body Work

ONE OF THE BIGGEST CHALLENGES for survivors is to be comfortable with their bodies. The abuse taught us that our bodies are not our own, that we have no control over what happens to our bodies, and we may even feel that our bodies have betrayed us.

One of the best practices that I developed to overcome this challenge is yoga. I started yoga when my husband and I decided we wanted to start a family. I learned that it is best not to start any new physical practice once you are pregnant. So, being the Type-A person I am, I started yoga as soon as possible.

There were several different hatha yoga studios available near where I lived when I first started yoga. I followed my usual approach: to use both a systematic method to narrow down the options and then rely on my gut feelings to make a final decision.

I researched the types of yoga each studio offered, saw which ones had classes scheduled for times I could attend with my work and graduate school schedule, and then visited the studios to talk with the teachers. When I walked into the Boca Yoga Iyengar studio, this intuitive feeling struck me that it was a safe place and I would be happy there. Talking with a teacher sealed the deal for me; he was so gentle and kind to me.

Dealing with Triggers in Yoga Practice

I started beginning classes, Level 1 in the Iyengar tradition, which is an alignment-based yoga system that uses props and commonly has many variations of a pose that allow for students' physical capabilities. I saw yoga as a tool to get my body into shape for pregnancy. Over time, it became obvious that my husband and I were not destined to have a family, but I kept up with the yoga practice because it made me feel better physically. But I noticed my anxiety in certain poses, especially ones like Happy Baby pose (Ananda Balasana) that left me feeling exposed. No "happy baby" for me!

I realized certain poses triggered me and finally sat down and spoke to my yoga instructor. Never having talked about my abuse with anyone outside of family, friends, or therapists, it was a big leap for me to open up to the teacher. It turned out that his father sexually abused his sister, so he understood of the impacts of sexual abuse.

He was wonderful about being supportive of me, and we decided together that I would not have to do certain poses and that he would provide alternative poses in class for me when I felt uncomfortable..

Although at first I felt I would stand out by being in poses different from other students in the class, he reassured me that the yoga studio was a safe place of nonjudgement. I discovered I could continue the work I enjoyed without having to feel like everyone would see I was a "special case" that had to be treated differently. I wouldn't have to feel like an outsider this time. And I experienced a slow appreciation of my body in a new way.

Transforming My Relationship with My Body

During the years of abuse, at a deep level, I always thought my body was betraying me. That somehow my body "encouraged" the unwanted attention by my grandfather. And especially confusing were the pleasurable body sensations that accompanied the abuse coupled with the feeling of horrible wrongness of what he was doing to me.

As I described earlier, I enjoyed athletic activities like basketball because they made me feel strong, confident, and in control of my body. At that time, to me my body was just a machine that could do what I asked of it. I could be a part of sports teams in school that fed my need to belong and seem normal, providing me many fun experiences because my body was strong and fit.

I skirted on the edge of anorexia while in high school. I monitored the amount of food I ate, but that was balanced by the drive to stay healthy to play sports. Always a skinny kid, I think subconsciously I tried to minimize the amount of hormone-driven change happening to me as my body started to transform. Luckily, at that time my metabolism was so high that I could stay skinny easily without starving myself.

Before starting a yoga practice, I saw my body as something to maintain: feed the machine, tune the machine, and it will perform the way I needed when active. Once I started yoga, I began to consider my body as a partner with my emotions and feelings. Somehow, for all those years before yoga, I perceived my body as

71

being the victim of my stress and emotional highs and lows. Stress led to headaches and muscle pain, stomach issues, and insomnia.

With yoga, I started to experience a reintegration of my body with my emotions. I began to see my body as both strong and flexible, having both stamina and the ability for experiencing subtle nuances of movement and feeling. My body was not only the victim of emotional turmoil but it was an active participant in a dialog with my emotional and mental experiences. I began to reconnect with areas of my body that I'd rejected, to appreciate the gifts my body could give to me. It has been a profoundly transformative experience and I continue my practice in classes and at home to this day.

Your Yoga Practice

I recommend yoga highly as a practice for your journey of healing from sexual abuse. It will provide a good physical exercise for your body but more importantly, the poses will help you to more fully connect with your body.

The growing awareness of the benefits of yoga in treating trauma and PSTD has led to the development of trauma-informed yoga practices.

"Trauma-informed yoga isn't a cure, but it can provide healing to people dealing with trauma, as well as tools to cope with their emotional scars while boosting their physical well-being."

Learn more at https://health.usnews.com/well-ness/mind/articles/2017-03-29/how-yoga-helps-survivors-of-trauma

I recommend researching the various yoga opportunities the way I did. Get online and find out what yoga is available in your area. Yoga classes are taught in many locations, including yoga studios, the YMCA, gyms, community centers, and wellness centers, to name a few.

YogaJournal.com has a directory, https://directory.yogajournal.com, that can help you find a yoga studio, and their site also has information on online classes and retreats.

Look for classes for beginners, or classes noted as "gentle," "restorative," or "chair" yoga. Even if you are physically fit, this is a new physical practice, and it is best to start off slowly.

See what classes the locations offer and find out what fits into your life and schedule. Then physically check out the locations and the teachers, and speak with the teachers to choose a class.

Also check for video classes online. Youtube.com is a great resource for free yoga videos by all kinds of yoga teachers. But a quick internet search will help you locate other options, such as apps for your phone or tablet.

Consider whether you need to have a teacher who is the opposite sex from your abuser. Working with a teacher of the same sex as your abuser may trigger you during class. Luckily, the male teachers I met at my first studio were so kind, gentle, and understanding that I felt safe being in their care.

Different amounts of direct interaction between students and teachers occur in the different types of yoga when you attend a class physically. Yoga classes may involve physical adjustments of the students by the teacher to help the students get into the poses more accurately or fully. You are perfectly within your rights to ask the teacher how much adjusting is done in class without revealing anything about your abuse history.

But, if you are comfortable sharing your abuse history, you could ask the teacher how much experience they have in working with survivors and how they would help you during class when you are anxious or triggered by certain poses.

Rely on your intuition to decide which yoga class and teacher will be best for you. And if it turns out that the first teacher or location is not a good fit, find a teacher and/or location that works for you. (And if you are watching videos online, it is a simple thing to move on to another teacher's offerings.)

Other Types of Body Work

If you feel that yoga might not be the best practice for you, you might consider other body work practices. Tai chi and qigong are traditional Chinese forms of exercise. I incorporate qigong in my daily healing journey practices and find it helpful physically and mentally. The deep breathing and slow, deliberate-moving postures help keep my stress low and my anxiety in check.

If You're Not Ready for a Group Setting

You may not be ready to work with your body in a group setting. Your body image and how you see yourself may be such that you don't want anyone else to see you doing physical activity or while you are dressed in clothes for working out. You may feel too exposed or vulnerable to do a new physical activity in front of other people. Then you can consider purchasing a yoga, tai chi, or qigong video so you can practice at home in private. Amazon.com has many options for reasonable prices. Numerous classes are also available for free online, such as on Youtube.com

I recommend you start with a "gentle" yoga DVD or online class, or a DVD or online class for beginners for any of the forms. My favorite is a DVD set from Yoga Journal: "Yoga Journal: 21 Day Challenge Transform Your Body in 3 Weeks." I use these sessions in my daily morning practice. I don't follow the twenty-one-day program as presented, necessarily, but pick the particular sessions that work for me where I am at the time.

Also, you can consider bodywork practices that are "receptive" rather than active, such as:

- **Massage:** the therapeutic practice of manipulating the muscles and limbs to ease tension and reduce pain.
- **Reiki:** a healing technique based on the principle that the therapist can channel energy into the patient, by means of touch, to activate the natural healing processes of the patient's body and restore physical and emotional well-being.
- **Energy medicine:** the act of channeling and manipulating the energy that courses through your body in order to heal it.
- **Chakra healing:** a form of Ayurvedic medicine that facilitates the even flow of energy through seven energy centers located in the central body.
- **Acupuncture:** a form of Chinese medicine that involves pricking the skin or tissues with needles, used to alleviate

pain and to treat various physical, mental, and emotional conditions.

Online searches for these bodywork practices will help you find practitioners in your area.

Before starting any new physical activity, it is always good to discuss your plans with your primary care doctor.

Finding a Class that Works for You

Below are questions to guide you in documenting the various types of classes, the places and times where you can attend a class, and the teacher's credentials/training for each yoga studio or online yoga practice you are interested in. Write the answers in your notebook/journal. Also include notes about your thoughts and feelings about the space and the teacher.

If you will be attending a physical class outside your home, I recommend going to a location and speaking with a potential teacher before starting a class.

- Is an organization providing the class? Or is this a private offering by an individual, certified teacher?
- Type of class (of yoga/tai chi/ qigong)?
- Location (near work or home, or virtual?)
- Class days and time (Do they fit with your work and home schedule, or are they available as recordings you can watch later?)

Teacher's credentials and years of experience. What are your thoughts after talking with the teacher if you are able to connect with them directly?

Meditation and Contemplation

TWO OF THE MOST HELPFUL PRACTICES I developed in my healing journey are the related activities of meditation and contemplation. Meditation is training the mind through a set of techniques to attain mental clarity and focus and emotional stability and calm. Contemplation is deep reflective thought where you consider something carefully for an extended period. These can be words, phrases, ideas, or passages in spiritual or inspirational texts.

Several techniques are available for meditation, including focusing your attention on a single object, like your breath; affirmations; loving-kindness meditation, using mantras or sounds; and guided meditations, guided imagery, relaxation, or body scanning.

All the major world religions, including Christianity, Judaism, Buddhism, and Hinduism, have meditation and/or contemplative practices as part of their traditional spiritual practices.

My Early Meditation Practices

My particular experiences have been in Buddhist and Christian practices. I initially engaged with Buddhist mindfulness-awareness meditation that is a seated meditation where the focus of the meditation is the breath. As active as my mind can be, it was challenging to sit for periods of time and keep in touch with my breath.

I started with guided meditation practices by Jon Kabat-Zinn and Thich Nhat Hanh. As I continued on my healing journey, I found several other wonderful teachers who have been helpful in developing my meditation practices: Pema Chödrön, Deepak Chopra, Tara Brach, Susan Piver, Jack Kornfield, and Sharon Salzberg. See the notes at the end of the chapter for more information on these teachers.

I decided I wanted a more personal and in-person meditation experience, so I joined the Shambhala Meditation Center in Atlanta (SMCA), which has a beautiful meditation room with wood floors and lots of windows to let in natural light. Through regular attendance to group meditation sessions, classes, workshops, and retreats, I slowly learned how to let go of my need to rehash the past and excessively worry about and plan for the future, at least when on the cushion! I also started an at-home meditation practice in the mornings, which I continue to this day, as part of my yoga practice, to give my mind the opportunity for quiet and peace before starting my day.

Contemplative Arts

I was introduced to Contemplative Art practices as a member of the SMCA. These are art practices, such as calligraphy, Ikebana (Japanese art of flower arrangement), and contemplative photography, where the goal is to use the creative to synchronize the mind and body in the present moment. It isn't about the particular contemplative art you are engaged with, but the state of the mind while doing the practices. These are practices because each of the art forms is based on instructions, exercises, and processes that provide a container for the development of the contemplative state of mind.

Art and the Brain

Exposure to visual art and participation in creative activities creates positive brain changes.

Over thirty years of scientific investigation have demonstrated that creative expression can alter not just moods, attitudes and emotions, but influences neuro-endocrine pathways that control physiologic outcomes as varied as blood pressure, sleep and the immune response.

We are learning how creative expression can:

• reduce blood pressure while boosting the immune system and reducing stress

• promote relaxation and a sense of well-being

• reduce anxiety, depression, and pain

• promote general quality of life by putting individuals in touch with their feelings and providing a means to express this to others.

https://www.artandhealing.org/art-healing-ptsd

A description of a number of contemplative art practices can be found at https://shambhala.org/programs/contemplative-arts/.

I studied Ikebana and contemplative photography, taking classes, doing workshops, and engaging in my own personal practices. I fell in love with contemplative photography because it got me out into the world of nature and connected me with the beauty of the world through my camera. I eventually went through training to become a certified teacher so I could share this wonderful practice with others.

Impact on My Healing Journey

My meditation practice and contemplative photography practices have been an integral part of my healing journey. Meditation helped me learn that I was not the voice of negativity clamoring loudly in my head. I learned how to release my attachment to the negative self-talk, to relax out of the stress of beating myself up about the past and fearing the future.

I learned to recognize and truly see the behavior patterns that I engaged in automatically—patterns that may have served me as a child to protect myself but now were no longer serving me as an adult. My photography practice helped me get grounded so I could open to my strengths and capabilities rather than being boxed in by old patterns and fears.

Great meditation teachers are out there. My experience with meditation is mostly through the Buddhist tradition, but opportunities are also available for learning meditation instruction in other secular organizations and religious traditions.

In the Resources section of the book, I have listed several of the teachers I have learned from in reading their books or listening to their video lectures or classes. They offer slightly different approaches to meditation, one of which might resonate with you.

All of these teachers have wonderful insights available on their websites. Many of them also have blogs and newsletters. You can find instructional videos on their websites and Youtube.com. Their books about the meditation practice are available from their websites and from retailers, such as Amazon.

Several meditation apps are available for your phone and other devices. I have provided a list of several popular meditation apps in the Resources section of the book.

Your Meditation Practice

Meditation is challenging to do, so you don't want to give up too soon if you encounter roadblocks to your progress. But you also need to be mindful of when the meditation practice is aggravating or intensifying your symptoms and stop when needed.

A Special Note for Those Trying Meditation

Many meditation techniques ask you to pay close, continued attention to your internal experiences.

When you do so, you may encounter thoughts, memories, or physical sensations that are coupled with your abuse experience.

If you are meditating on your own, it might be better to stop that meditation practice and find an alternative practice, such as guided meditation or mantra/sound meditation.

If you are doing meditation one-on-one with an instructor or in a group meditation practice, speak with the meditation instructor about your experience with the meditation and how it is triggering you. See if they have suggestions for you.

Write your answers to the following questions in your notebook/journal.

- Are you wanting to try meditation on your own in your own home?
- If yes, then consider checking out the meditation teachers above. Which ones do you think are offering

instruction that resonates with you? Are you able to watch a video, purchase a book or online class from them that can introduce you to meditation?

- What types of meditation instruction can you find on youtube.com, udemy.com or other online resources that resonate with you?
- Or, are you wanting to try meditation with a group to receive in-person instruction?

If yes, then note the types of meditation classes, the places and times where you can attend a class, and the teacher's credentials/training in your notebook/journal. Also note information about your thoughts and feelings on the space and the teacher. I recommend going to a location and speaking with a potential teacher before starting a class if you are planning to attend a class in person.

- Is an organization providing the class? Or is this a private offering by an individual certified meditation teacher?
- What type of meditation is being offered? For what level of student?
- Location (near work or home, or virtual?)
- Class Days and Time (Do they fit with your work and home schedule, or are they available as recordings you can watch later?)
- Teacher's credentials, years of experience, and your thoughts after talking with the teacher if you are able to connect with them directly.

CHAPTER 10

Being in Nature

I FOUND THAT GETTING OUT INTO NATURE is healing. When we lived in Florida, I would spend time on the weekends walking along the beaches in the morning as the sun rose. The combination of the sand beneath my feet, the sun on my face and body, the wind through my hair, and the sound of the waves rolling into the beach were all balms to release my anxiety, fear, and self-deprecating thoughts.

I could feel the energy flowing around me with the sights and sounds of nature. And being there early meant there were fewer people to distract me and make me self-conscious about what I was wearing or how I looked. I felt I could relax my guard and be present to see the sunrise and watch the various birds play at the water's edge.

I also visited the Morikami Museum and Japanese Gardens, a wonderful place with a series of gardens progressing through the history of traditional planned gardens of Japan. Again, I would go early to beat the heat and the crowds and wander my way through the various gardens, stopping every so often to sit on a beach and contemplate the wonderful views.

I still find that identifying a way to get outside and experience nature is one of the best ways to keep my head on straight and to let go of things that can weigh heavily on my mind or bring me down emotionally.

How I Connect to Nature

I don't have to make big plans to go on a camping trip or vacation to exotic places. I don't have to set up an elaborate travel schedule or have to spend a lot of money. I don't even have to take time off of work. I only need to make a bit of time for myself to get out and away from my routine. A half-hour or an hour or two is enough time to recharge and re-energize.

It doesn't matter where I find that slice of nature. If it's a small grassy space or empty field near where I live, that's a good start. It can be a city park with open grassy areas and a few trees. It can be a botanical or botanic garden, an arboretum, a state park or national park. Even going to the local zoo can get me out and feeling connected to nature.

I often take my camera with me or use the camera on my cell phone to capture the beautiful moments I experience while out on my walks. This helps me to slow down mentally and allows me to open up, with curiosity, to what I might find as I am moving through the space.

Sometimes I want to be by myself and uninterrupted by other people. Those are times I look for places where there will be fewer people around, like the arboretum. Often, I go as soon as the gardens or parks open so I will be there before the crowds arrive. The added benefit is that the morning energy is fantastic, and the light is wonderful for photographing!

If I am at a place with few people, I let myself wander aimlessly, without an agenda, exploring the space and seeing what I find along the way. If it's a planned space, I grab a map ahead of time to help me see what is there to explore. I leverage a map app on my phone to help me find my way back to my car in case I wander beyond where I recognize the way back.

Sometimes I don't feel like being by myself. I want to be out with people but not interact with them. Then I will choose a place where I can expect people to be, like the gardens or parks on a weekend afternoon. I can still do my wandering approach to explore the space, but now I can also add some people-watching.

Regardless of whether I am being alone in a space or in a space filled with people, I will take time to sit and absorb the sounds, sights, and smells as they arise. Many of the gardens and parks I visit have benches. I can sit in the sun or shade, my choice, and absorb what is happening around me.

I love listening to the birds singing, or the breezes moving the leaves in the trees in quiet places. Or dogs barking, people calling to each other, the sounds of their play in crowded spaces. My favorite botanical garden has a large wind chime by a shaded swinging bench that is a fantastic place to sit and simply be for a while.

And when the weather is bad, I will go online to find nature videos on Youtube.com, many of which include soothing music.

"The idea that spending time in nature can make you feel better is intuitive ...

"People who have been suffering from stress, sickness, or a trauma can spend quiet contemplative time in gardens or taken to the mountains or woods to heal. But nature is not just wilderness. The benefits of nature can also be found in our communities' parks and green spaces. Researchers are amassing a body of evidence [that proves] what we all know to be true: nature is good for us and has both long and short term mental and physical health benefits."

Check out hundreds of free research studies, news articles, and case studies, organized by adult and children health topics at

https://www.asla.org/healthbenefitsofnature.aspx

How You Can Connect with Nature

Write the answers to the following questions in your notebook/journal for each space you want to explore.

Where can you go to find the peace in nature?

- Name of space near you
- Type of space (park, garden, arboretum, zoo)
- Location (near work or home?)

- Days and times open (do they fit with your week/week-end schedule?)
- Quiet space or people-busy space?
- Can you go early to miss the crowds?
- Can you go later to join the crowds?
- Any special events to know about at the space?

Creative Expression

OPENING MYSELF TO BEING CREATIVE has been a major part of my healing journey. I have found several creative outlets over the years that have helped me express what happened to me as a child and connect back to being artistic for the fun and joy of it.

I recommend doing art as part of your healing journey. A survivor of childhood abuse is often forced to grow up quickly, even to the point of denying their child self. Doing art and creative activities can help reconnect to that child self and also provide healing for that child self. Even if your sexual abuse happened after your childhood, connecting with your creativity can still be an opportunity to support your healing journey through playfulness and creative expression.

My Creative Journey

I was very creative as a child: drawing and writing poetry and short stories. But I silenced my inner artist by comparing myself to others and deciding that I wasn't as good as they were so I couldn't be an artist or creative. Then school took over my mental energy and time, and I put all thoughts of being creative aside. I experienced a short bout of creativity in graduate school doing black-and-white and nature photography when my dad gifted me his camera, but I soon set it aside to immerse myself in my studies.

My creativity bloomed again while living in Florida. I was drawn to the beaches there, particularly early in the day with the sun rising and few people around. I would walk and create poems about what I saw, felt, and experienced on the beach. After creating several poems in my head, I would rush to my car and write them down on scrap paper. I later published a series of those poems with illustrations by a fellow artist, Nancy Standlee. "Dreams of the Turtle King" available on exclusively on Amazon.com.   https://www.amazon.com/Dreams-Turtle-King-Inspired-Florida-ebook/dp/B00H5CZNCQ

I also started doing yoga at that same time, which opened me up to the heartache and painful memories of the abuse. The beach inspired my creativity for writing playful and inspirational poems, which connected me with writing on my morning walks. That connection enabled me to put pen to paper and capture my feelings and experiences about the abuse and my healing journey to that point. I would write my beach poems in the morning and write about the abuse and my healing journey at night. I include the poems about my abuse and healing journey that I wrote during that time as Part IV in this book. My hope is for some of them to inspire your creativity as part of your own healing journey.

Contemplative Photography

I later connected again with photography. Living in Atlanta and attending the SMCA, I learned about the Miksang Contemplative Photography practice. It is a contemplative practice using a camera to slow down and connect more directly with the world. I fell in love with Miksang, taking all the workshops and eventually becoming a certified teacher to share the practice with others.

My contemplative photography practice has brought endless beauty and appreciation into my life. The abuse had pushed me into a mental realm where only fear and a sense of ugliness existed; ugliness about what was out in the world, ugliness about what the world and the people in it would do to me, and ugliness I felt about myself.

Contemplative photography opened a window in my soul to feel connected with the world and the beauty always right around me. It gave me a way to slow down to see the beauty, and to use my camera to capture it and make it a part of myself. It gave me a way to share that beauty with other people through the images I shot and the classes I taught. There is nothing like giving the gift of beauty to yourself and other people to bring joy into your life!

Doing contemplative photography gets me outside into nature and the world and also gets me outside of my normal criticizing and self-doubting mind. For a time, I can let go of any storyline and open myself up to the beauty and wonder of the ordinary world. And I have beautiful images to enjoy and share later!

Art Therapy

If you are looking to experience structured art in a therapeutic setting, specially trained therapists offer art therapy. Art therapy "use[s] art media, the creative process, and the resulting artwork to explore [clients'] feelings, reconcile emotional conflicts, foster self-awareness, manage behavior and addictions, develop social skills, improve reality orientation, reduce anxiety, and increase self-esteem."[3]

The healing power of art has long been recognized by artists around the world, but it is now emerging as an evidence-based therapeutic modality for a number of different mental health conditions, including trauma, PTSD, depression.[1]

Art therapy excels for body work because clients manipulate artwork outside themselves. By externalizing difficult pieces of their trauma stories, clients begin to safely access their physical experiences and relearn that their bodies are a safe place.[2]

[1] https://www.psycom.net/iwar-1-html/art-therapy-and-trauma
[2] https://www.healthline.com/health/art-therapy-for-ptsd#PTSD,-the-body,-and-art-therapy

[3] https://www.arttherapy.org/upload/whatisarttherapy.pdf

94

If you are interested in exploring art therapy with a trained art therapist, check out the Art Therapist Locator at https://art-therapy.org/art-therapist-locator.

SoulCollage®

Fortunately, I discovered SoulCollage® recently. "Originated by Seena Frost, SoulCollage® is a process for accessing your intuition and creating an incredible deck of cards with deep personal meaning that will help you with life's questions and transitions."[4].

I heard about SoulCollage® from an artist friend, and we took a workshop together. SoulCollage® works with images from a variety of resources—magazines, books, photographs, drawings, and more. My photographer side went nuts when I found another practice that uses images!

SoulCollage® is a real wonder because it allows you to bypass the analytic, critical part of your brain to tap into the intuitive, creative part of your brain. Cutting and gluing the images down together to make a card is playful and fun. The journaling work with the collage you have created is revealing and taps into deeper, bigger wisdom than you realized you had access to. I have learned a lot and healed a lot working with my cards.

This year I am challenging myself to explore more types of art. I have taken classes in gelatin hand printing, acrylic pour painting, silk painting, and indigo dyeing. I love working with different mediums and letting my creativity flow and play. I have even starting doing classes shared by artists online and finding interesting art videos on Youtube.com.

---

[4] https://soulcollage.com

Journaling

Journaling is a powerful healing practice. Whether you write in poetry or prose, your writing is structured or you write as a stream of consciousness, you can use journaling as a safe place to let out all the emotions you are feeling. You can write your story, write out how you see it and feel it.

Not only can it be a tool to feel and release your feelings of anger, resentment, fear, shame, or guilt, but it can also be a way to identify patterns of behavior, your specific challenges or triggers, and bring perspective to help your healing journey. It can also be a place to capture things you are grateful for during your healing journey. And it can be a great resource in working with your therapist.

"Whatever event, habit, or disorder you are struggling to overcome, journaling can help you find healing."

"If you are suffering in the aftermath of a traumatic event, journaling can help you find the good in life."

See the extensive research supporting the healing power of journaling at:
https://positivepsychology.com/benefits-of-journaling/

Connecting to Your Creativity

You can connect to your creativity through journaling and writing. You can do it through photography. You can do it through crocheting, sewing, knitting, quilting, or needlepoint. You can do it through art classes for drawing, painting, pottery, or jewelry making, woodworking, sculpting, or blacksmithing! You can do it by visiting art museums, going to the theater, or seeing shows. Whatever sparks your creativity is something to bring more of into your life!

Read through the questions below and write your answers in your notebook/journal.

- How would you like to (re-)connect to your creativity? Through writing, journaling, visual arts, fine arts, crafts or something else?
- Are there art museums in your area you can visit?
- Are there art classes you can take at a local museum, arts & craft store, community center, local art studios, or through adult education centers, local art league, or art group?
- Are there art or writing classes you can take online? Or Youtube.com videos you can watch and learn from for your favorite kind of art?

Pampering Yourself

I SPENT A LOT OF TIME PUNISHING MYSELF early in my life before I understood what had happened to me and why I felt the way I did about myself and my body. I would belittle myself, mentally and out loud. I would push myself and ignore my body's messages for nutrition and hydration. I would use eating to control myself.

I never developed bulimia nervosa or anorexia nervosa, but I skipped meals regularly and would use food as a reward for doing things well at school. I didn't consciously think about using eating as a control and reward system, but that was my relationship with food. I disliked my body, but I wanted to be fit enough to do things that brought me enjoyment, like bicycling, marching band, and basketball.

My basketball coach encouraged me to gain weight so I would be better able to play my position as a center and not get pushed around so much by stronger, heavier girls. My mom took me to a doctor who showed me how much I would have to eat to gain the weight I wanted—a 3,000 calorie-a-day diet. I could not imagine eating that much food every day, so it didn't go anywhere. Needless to say, I stayed a tall, skinny girl throughout school.

Healing My Relationship with My Body

Getting to a place where I felt I deserved to be happy and feel good about my body took a long time and a lot of work. I wasted so many years punishing myself and my body because of how bad I felt about myself and my sense of my body's betrayal. It took a drastic shift in my thinking to believe I "deserved" good things, to be kind to my body and to appreciate it. To realize it was a great gift to treat myself as I would treat a dear friend.

As I progressed along my healing journey and developed a healthier relationship with my body, I began to appreciate what it could do for me when I treated it well. And I learned how it would impact me if I didn't treat myself well or if I let myself get overwhelmed by stress and anxiety. The stress and anxiety are still often a challenge when "out of my control" things happen, but now I have a repertoire of activities I can do to support or even pamper myself.

Learning how not to go overboard from punishing to the opposite direction of overindulging also took time. But eventually, I found the balance and the body-intelligence to know when I needed a special treat for myself and how to bring enjoyable and pampering things into my life on a regular basis.

Pampering through Massage, Spas, and Resorts

I enjoy a good massage. I still am not comfortable getting down to my underwear or even naked to be touched by a strange man, even a licensed massage therapist, so I get massages from women. I even had a hard time letting strange women touch me in the beginning, but being in a place with relaxing music, a gentle touch, and nice heated tables is now a wonderful treat!

I enjoy a day at a spa getting facials, pedicures, and manicures. It is not something I do very often, but it is a pampering event for me to book a full day at a spa to let everyone treat me like a VIP and take care of me. Usually, it's a local spa, but every so often I make it a minivacation to get away and be pampered.

I also like to go on retreats. These can be yoga retreats, meditation retreats, photography retreats, women's retreats—whatever captures my interest at that time in my life and something I know will be relaxing, enjoyable, and indulging. They can be challenging as well, but I mostly find them energizing and healing.

Given the expense of massages, and particularly spa days and retreats that are more rare pampering events, I try to find less expensive ways to pamper myself and my body.

DIY Pampering

I relish a nice, hot bubble bath with essential oils, which I can get easily from chain stores or online shopping. It is wonderful to ease into a hot, sweet-smelling bath to read a good book or watch a nice video or movie.

I also love scented candles. They are a great addition to a hot bath, but I also like to enjoy scented candles when I am working on the computer or reading a book in bed. Same thing with incense. My husband has asthma, so I have to use the candles when he is at work.

Please be aware that some scents (including essential oils, pot-pourri, air fresheners, and candles) can be toxic for pets.

Learn more at
https://www.preventivevet.com/cats/scents-that-are-harmful-to-your-pets

I also feel like I'm pampering myself when I buy beautiful flowers. My husband will get me flowers now and again. But any time I like, I can pop into the grocery store to pick up a small bouquet of bright flowers. I usually put them on the kitchen counter and the kitchen table so I can enjoy them whenever I am in the kitchen or living room.

It may seem strange to consider that pampering, but I see it as a way of treating my eyes and my nose with the flowers' beauty and fragrance. I can do that for myself without having to wait on anyone else to do it for me.

And let's not forget chocolate! I am a chocoholic and love dark chocolate, especially with nuts. My husband often buys me chocolates of all kinds to pamper me ... sometimes a little too often for my desire to maintain my weight, but he knows how to feed my craving. Especially with those Girl Scout cookies! Thanks, honey!

I entered our relationship with a love of milk chocolate and a strong dislike of dark chocolate. That dislike may have come from trying to sneak the cooking chocolate from my grand-mother's pantry as a kid. But my husband got the mistaken idea that I loved dark chocolate and kept buying me various dark chocolate candies and bars. I didn't have the heart to tell him I didn't like it because he was being so sweet to me. Eventually, he converted me so that now I love dark chocolate over milk chocolate!

My past issues with using food for control and reward is something I stay aware of, but I let myself enjoy chocolate for the simple reason that it tastes good and makes me feel good. And now there is evidence that dark chocolate is good for you! According to WebMD and Medical News today, it is nutritious with soluble fiber and minerals and is loaded with antioxidants. It may improve blood flow, lower blood pressure, reduce heart disease, raise HDL (cholesterol), lower the risk of diabetes, protect your skin from sun damage, and improve your brainpower.[5,6] Wow! See how many reasons I have to be a chocoholic?

But in all seriousness, I have found ways to treat my body and its various senses in ways that are enjoyable and nurturing. And I have found ways to do that as extra special treats and frequent gifts to myself. It's never too late to find the things that make you feel pampered.

Pampering Yourself

Write the answer to the questions below in your notebook/journal.

- How can you pamper yourself today? What would you find enjoyable?

---

[5] https://www.webmd.com/diet/health-benefits-dark-chocolate#
[6] https://www.medicalnewstoday.com/articles/dark-chocolate

- What could you do for an extra special treat for yourself?
- What type of spa or retreat would you enjoy?
- Is it something you would do with a friend or friends or just by yourself?
- What can you do that is inexpensive and you can do at home?
- How can you pamper your skin?
- How can you pamper your sense of smell?
- How can you pamper your visual sense, your eyes?
- How can you pamper your sense of taste?
- How can you pamper your sense of hearing?

Giving to Others

I SPENT A LOT OF TIME living in the past, in my head, when I started remembering the abuse. The memories and effects of the abuse were so overwhelming that I felt stuck in the past and constantly fighting demons.

One healing activity I discovered was to give of myself to others. I was not comfortable volunteering to work with sexual abuse-related groups because I feared being triggered by trying to help people directly overcome their abuse. But I found I could give of myself, my time, and my money in other ways that made a positive impact on my life and the lives of others.

Giving Back During My Healing Journey

In graduate school, I joined a program called Voices for Children. We were trained to assist families who had a *guardian ad litem* appointed by the courts to act as the representative for minor children. I also volunteered to read the newspaper to a woman who had limited vision and to tutor undergraduates who had learning challenges and needed extra support in their classes.

Once I entered the workforce, I tried to continue giving to others. I did my research and found charities that helped causes and groups important to me. I donate money to environmental focused groups, like the World Wildlife Fund (WWF), groups helping animals, like the International Primate Protection League and Dogs for Better Lives, and groups helping people like Charity Water.

I've used CharityNavigator.org many times over the years to help identify quality organizations to support. Even if I can only give a small amount of money to these organizations, I do what I can to lend my support.

I looked for ways to give of my time and skills and money. I have participated in being a judge for various scholarship offerings for nonprofit organizations. I have also been a volunteer speaker for conferences and events for STEM programs.

I support my church in a variety of ways. I've been the social media chair for maintaining their website and posting on social media. I give classes on meditation and contemplative arts. I am trained as a prayer chaplain and act as a greeter on Sunday mornings. I have facilitated a weekly book study. I have been a member of the board.

Impact of Giving

Each of these activities over the years has helped focus my attention on helping others and creating an energy of light in the world to replace the energy of darkness that came out of the abuse. These activities help me connect with others and nurture the side of myself that is generous, giving, and compassionate.

It helps me focus on the good things I can do in the world, the joy I can experience and share with others, and that means less energy and mind space are given over to the thoughts and feelings that arise from the past. I do not use these activities to distract myself but to balance the scale and to transform my thinking from painful, past-centered to joyful, in-the-now living.

As Winston Churchill said, "We make a living by what we get. We make a life by what we give."

Your Giving Opportunities

So how can you give your time, talent, skills or money?

Write your answers in your notebook/journal.

- What are your interests? What are you passionate about?
- Do you want to volunteer in person, or do online / virtual volunteering, or both?
- What skills and experience can you offer?
- Are you interested in learning a new skill or sharpening your skills? What tasks do you NOT like to do?
- How much time do you have to share?
- How flexible are your hours for volunteering?
- Do you want to work alone or in a group?
- Do you want a one-time assignment, a short-term assignment, or an ongoing assignment?
- If you cannot donate your time and talents, can you donate money to help an organization or group?
- What types of groups would you like to support monetarily? Local groups or national or international groups?

Part III: FIGURING IT OUT AND MOVING FORWARD

The next part of the book will focus on the difficult questions I asked myself along my healing journey, and how I found ways to move beyond the effects of the abuse.

DENISE BOSSARTE

Who Knew What and When?

I STRUGGLED A LONG TIME trying to understand who might have known about the abuse. Did my grandmother, the wife of my abuser, know about the abuse? Did my parents, particularly my mother, the daughter of my abuser, know about the abuse? Did anyone else in my family know?

When my abuser died while I was in high school, the memories of the abuse resurfaced. Because he died before I fully understood the abuse memories, I did not have to face the decision about whether to confront him and did not have to spend time around him after I remembered what he had done to me.

And then for a long time, I was too busy dealing with the overwhelming emotional trauma to ask myself questions about who might have known about what was happening to me. But then I got to the point I could feel anger about the abuse, and I started to ask who might have known. Who might have known and not done anything to stop it?

Considering My Parents

I wondered whether my grandfather had abused his daughters, whether my mother was a victim like me. But I was reluctant to say anything to my parents because I thought it might be the straw that broke the camel's back.

My parents were not doing well in their relationship at the time, and I didn't want to be the one to break them apart. I thought my father might blame my mother for not knowing, for taking us to my grandparent's house each summer and leaving us there alone with my abuser. And I worried that sharing my story might trigger my mom's remembering abuse by her father if she was abused.

Considering My Cousin

I have two female cousins, and for a long time I wondered whether they were abused too.

When I started reading *The Courage to Heal: A Guide for Women Survivors of Sexual Abuse* by Ellen Bass and Laura Davis in college, I finally reached out to my older cousin to share with her about what I remembered. I learned that our grandfather had also abused her. And that she knew our grandfather had raped her mother, my mother's older sister, at least one time.

She told me that when I was a child, she had seen my personality abruptly change from an open, demonstrably loving, happy child to a quiet, withdrawn, unhappy child. She had told herself that our grandfather must have gotten to me. She was in high school when she realized this.

At the time of her revelation, I was happy to have someone else who understood what I went through and what I was suffering now that the memories had returned. It wasn't until later that I wondered why she hadn't saved me from him.

Considering My Sister

For years I wondered if my sister was also a victim. Was she going through abuse like me? And later I wondered if she had any memories of what had happened to her.

After many years of work on my healing journey, I finally told my sister what had happened. She believed me and was furious at my grandfather about what he had done. She did not have any memories, and she worried that something might have happened to her and that she was suppressing the memories.

Based on what I knew of her, her relationships, and how she was living her life, she wasn't showing signs I recognized as having been abused. I told her I didn't know whether she had been abused as well, but that she was lucky not to have the memories to deal with like me!

Considering My Grandmother

And then there was my grandmother, the wife of the abuser. After my grandfather died, my grandmother seemed to blossom. She moved out of the house they had lived in and where the abuse occurred. She moved in across the street from my parents and started a new life for herself in a new town.

I spent more time one-on-one with my grandmother over the years after my grandfather died. I came to know her as a smart, sweet, supportive, and generous person. I learned more about how my grandparents met, and what being married to him was like for my grandmother. Although my grandfather was not physically abusive to my grandmother, he was very domineering and controlling of her during their fifty-plus years of marriage.

I decided that I cherished the relationship we developed when I became an adult and I didn't want the past abuse to come between us. I never told her what happened to me, and I never asked her what she knew.

A More Public Example of Abuse

Recently the systematic and decades-long abuse of female gymnasts by former doctor Larry Nassar came to light. The profound impact that the abuse had on so many girls sparked my desire to finally write my story and offer my lessons along my healing journey.

One thing stood out for me in the articles and testimonies. The statements that Larry Nassar would sexually abuse the girls while their moms and/or dads were present in the same room struck me. Nassar would position his body between the girls and their parents to hide the abuse.

If someone could be in the same room with a perpetrator *while* he was abusing his victim, how easy would it be to not know that something was happening to a child dropped off at her grandparents' house for the summer?

That helped me forgive what resentment or anger I carried for my family other than the person at fault—my grandfather.

Who Knew About Your Abuse?

Below are questions for exploring who knew what and when. These questions are ones that are best to discuss with your therapist so that they can work with you through the potentially triggering material.

Write your answers to the questions in your notebook/journal.

- Is it important for you to know who knew about the abuse?
- What will knowing do for you on your healing journey?
- If you find out members of your family or your friends knew, how will this impact your relationship with them?
- If you find out that others knew, others outside your family, how will that impact you and your healing journey?
- What advice does your therapist have for you about dealing with who knew what and when?

CHAPTER 15

Who Do I Tell?

DECIDING WHO TO SHARE YOUR STORY WITH can be one of the most difficult decisions of your healing journey.

When I first started to remember details of the abuse while in high school, many years before the #MeToo movement began, it terrified me that people would find out. I always felt like an outsider, different because I was bad, worthless, and unlovable. I did not understand before the memories resurfaced why I felt so bad about myself and my body. But when the memories came, they forced me to face the fact that now I knew. And my teenage brain believed that I was to blame for what had happened.

It horrified me that people would think less of me and would reject me for being tainted. I thought the only way to keep people from turning away from me was to hide what I was, a victim of incest. So besides the burden of knowing what had happened, I kept the BIG SECRET from everyone. And that made me feel more isolated than ever before.

Suicidal Thoughts

I did the best I could to hide my turmoil from my family and friends. I was not doing any healing, only suffering. I often had suicidal thoughts because the idea that I would feel so bad about myself for the rest of my life was unbearable. I wanted the emotional and psychological pain from the abuse to stop. I didn't know how to help myself get out of the pain, and sometimes I would consider what it would be like to be dead. I never went so far as to plan a specific method for killing myself, though I fantasized about cutting my wrists or turning on the car in the garage and just letting the exhaust fumes take me.

Sometime in elementary school, I convinced myself that I would be dead by age twenty-four. I don't know how I came up with that number and didn't know how it would happen, but I planted that seed for myself to have a deadline for when all the pain and anguish would stop. Some part of me wanted to live and was strong enough to keep me from trying to take my life but it took a few psychological games with my mind to keep myself going.

Hiding My Abuse

When I first started dating in high school, I kept my abuse to myself. When things became more intimate with my boyfriends, they would trigger the abuse memories. Depending on how close I was to that boyfriend emotionally and how much I trusted him, I would either try to ignore the triggered memory and "get through" the physical contact; I didn't want to appear to not like my boyfriends (which was like being victimized again). Or I would try to tell them I didn't want them to touch me there or in that way, saying nothing about why.

I was not close enough to other girls where I felt I could talk about how it felt to be intimate with boys. I didn't know if they enjoyed the physical intimacy, or if I was weird about how I was feeling. I was desperate for boys to like me and thereby prove I wasn't unlovable. I knew that if I told any of them the details of my abuse, they would drop me like a hot potato.

So with my boyfriends, I did a dance of intimacy and self-protection. I learned as a child to dissociate from my body while being abused, and I used that technique whenever I could not say no to intimate touching.

I kept my abuse from my mother and father for a long time. The experiences from my childhood had shown I could not trust my family to protect me. I got my grandfather's special attention, so I must have somehow caused it, and any suffering I experienced was my fault.

I extended my twisted concept of being to blame for my grandfather's actions to my mother being held accountable for my grandfather's actions. Maybe somewhere deep down I blamed my mother for not protecting me from her father, and that got pushed into how my parents would react. As a result, I held to my silence to keep from breaking up my parents' marriage. Funny how the mind works!

Finding the Courage to Share

As I got older, I became close to an older cousin. As I mentioned in the previous chapter, I shared with her about the abuse. It turned out that my grandfather also abused her. She never pressured me to tell anyone about the abuse that I was not ready to tell. She was supportive of me in a lot of ways, including encouraging me to get counseling help. Simply knowing that someone else had been abused helped ease any fears I had about making up any of the abuse but did not shift my thinking about myself or my body, and did not stop the feeling that I was responsible for what happened.

As a junior in college, I worked part time in a science lab. I started dating a graduate student doing his thesis work in the lab. He was a recovering alcoholic and regularly attended AA meetings. His openness in sharing about his addiction and how it affected his life before AA gave me the courage to share my abuse.

He was a wonderful gift from the universe to support me to truly begin my healing journey. He helped me find my first SIA meetings and supported me in getting help from my first therapist, which led to my first therapy group.

As I went through therapy in college, I gained enough understanding of my experiences to start believing I wasn't at fault. And the response my boyfriend gave, his loving support, gave me the courage to start sharing my history.

I wasn't ready to share with my parents yet, but I reached out to my sister to explain to her what had happened. I told her I would not tell our parents.

I still had lingering fears that it might impact their relationship, but I didn't want to deal with more people knowing. And I didn't want to be the one to trigger my mother's memories of abuse if she had been abused as well. I guess I didn't make it clear to my sister I didn't want *her* telling our parents because the next thing I knew, she had told them.

Let me say what a surprise it was for me to learn in my next conversation with my parents that my sister had let the proverbial cat out of the bag. My mother was very angry with my grandfather. She had taken all the pictures she had of him and cut him out of each one. She said nothing about remembering being abused, and I didn't ask.

My father was very upset to think this had happened and they had not known about it. He was distressed to think of all the times they had left my sister and me there with our grandfather every summer.

I was angry at my sister for that betrayal of trust. But in some ways, I was relieved that I didn't have to keep that secret from my parents anymore. My parents' relationship survived learning about the abuse (gee, I didn't have as much destructive power as I thought!) and they were willing to support me in whatever I needed in my healing journey.

Over time, I could share more easily with my boyfriends, close friends, and eventually, my fiancé. I never made a "big announcement" to the world (before this book) because I did not feel I needed everyone to know. It was my private experience to share with people who had earned my trust to know something so intimate about me.

But each telling, each sharing, was received with empathy and understanding, and slowly I became comfortable with more people knowing.

I mentioned in the Creative Expression chapter how, while living in Florida, in the evenings I would write poems about my abuse. My husband encouraged me to publish those poems in a book because he thought they could help other survivors with their healing. At the time, I felt that no one would be interested in reading poems about my story and that the poetry by itself was not enough to publish. I lacked the courage to try. I did create a short chapbook of the poems and printed out a few of them to share with friends on my home computer. But I never went further with sharing my work.

Inspired by #MeToo and USA Female Gymnasts

When the #MeToo movement started, I was amazed by and proud of all the women stepping up to say what had happened to them. Everyone's courage was inspiring, and it encouraged me that the United States and beyond was now having to see, unavoidably, the impact sexual abuse has on women.

But I didn't feel that joining the #MeToo movement was for me. I am at a point in my healing journey that I didn't feel making a #MeToo announcement would further my healing. It didn't feel right for me. Just the same way that my friend and husband's encouragement to write a book to tell my story didn't feel right to me. It felt like the focus would be on the abuse itself, rather than on the healing from the abuse.

But then the stories kept coming out about how many women have been affected, and the story of the systematic and long-term abuse of the US female gymnasts broke. That's when I realized I had something to share of value; things that helped me on my healing journey that I thought could help others. So now is the time for me to share my story with the world.

Sharing Your Story

Who will you share your story with? That is completely up to you. I strongly encourage you to share your story with a therapist to help you on your healing journey. I also strongly encourage you to share with your partner if you are in a relationship, to include them in your healing journey; see the next chapter, "Partners," for more details.

But beyond that, who you tell should be *your* personal decision. If you feel that joining #MeToo and sharing your story in a public way on social media will be helpful in your healing, then go for it! But if you feel your story is something you only want to share with people you know who have earned your trust, then that is your right.

Me Too movement founder Tarana Burke said in her 2018 *New York Times* interview,

> What we're trying to do is [...] say, "You don't have to tell your story publicly. You don't have to tell anybody what happened to you." You have to get it out—but it doesn't have to be at a poetry reading. It doesn't have to be on social media at all. It could be a trusted friend. It could be your journal.[7]

What Comes Next?

As you go on your healing journey, you will need to make some tough decisions about the people and activities in your life. You may learn that certain people are not helping you on your healing journey. Some people may want you to stay the way you are and not change. They may not like that you are changing from the victim they have known. They ground this relationship in your victim mentality and approach to life.

Once you move toward being a Thriver, some people will resist your efforts to change. They may criticize you, make fun of you, or even try to make you question yourself and what you are

---

[7] https://www.nytimes.com/2018/10/15/arts/tarana-burke-me-too-anniversary.html

trying to do. They fear change and want to hold on to the old you as strongly as possible.

You might need to change what you share about yourself and your life with these people. You may need to change how much time you spend with these people, or you may even need to let these people go from your life. Despite what anyone may tell you, your healing needs to come first, and sometimes that means walking away from the people who won't support your journey.

This is not an easy decision to make or an easy thing to do. Some of these people may be spouses, children, families of origin, or close friends. These relationships are complicated and difficult to evaluate. That is where having a neutral person in your life, such as a therapist, can help you carefully and deliberately assess relationships to see whether they are neutral, enriching, or detrimental to your healing process.

Think about sharing your story. Whatever your decision, please make it one based on the thoughtful consideration of both short-term and long-term influences on your healing journey.

Who Do You Tell About Your Abuse?

Write your answers to the questions below in your notebook/journal.

- Is it important to you that people know about your abuse, or do you want to keep it private?
- What will sharing, or not, do for you on your healing journey?
- Is it possible that by sharing you can prevent this abuser from preying on others?

- If you are ready to share your story, who will you share it with?
- Why will you share it with these people and not others?
- How do you expect these people to react? What if they don't react as you hoped?
- Will you ask people to keep your story in confidence, or are you okay with them sharing it?
- Will you be okay if they share your story on the internet? What might happen if they share it without your permission?
- Are you considering joining #MeToo? If so, how will it help your healing journey?
- What if some people don't believe you? What if you are accused of being a liar?
- What if your friends, family, or coworkers demonize you or ostracize you when they learn your story?

• CHAPTER 16 •

Partners

SHARING WITH A PARTNER can be a very scary thing to consider, let alone do.

I decided to include a chapter about sharing with a partner because of their deeply intimate and important role. Sharing with a partner is different from sharing with anyone else, and I want to offer specific suggestions and questions for preparing for and actually sharing with this important person in your life.

I have shared my abuse with only a few of my partners over the years. I only shared with boyfriends I felt would be in my life longer-term and with whom I felt safe enough emotionally to share my experiences. I knew not all the people I dated would be able to handle what had happened to me. Each time I had a new relationship, I needed to decide about whether I was ready to share such a deep, foundational piece of myself.

Deep in the Shame

In the early years, I was still deeply embedded in the mentality that I was at fault; I was dirty, broken, damaged goods, and unlovable. I couldn't imagine that anyone would want me. When someone seemed interested in getting to know me and dating me, the last thing I wanted was for them to know about my abuse!

It was terrifying to think I would open myself up to a person I cared about and they might reject me for what had happened to me. I could barely tolerate myself; how could I expect anyone else to still want me or to be with me if they knew how rotten I was at the core?

I think back to that younger self and feel such compassion for how scared and isolated and damaged she felt. I don't think she made poor decisions about who she shared her experiences with, but I wish that the agony the decisions caused her was something she did not have to experience.

Sharing with Boyfriends

I shared what had happened to me with one boyfriend in high school. At that point, with my grandfather dying, the memories shoved deep down and locked away resurfaced with a vengeance.

Things got crazy during that time of my life both mentally and emotionally, and I was lucky that someone was there who could tell me it wasn't my fault and who was very gentle with me. He wasn't equipped to help me beyond not running away from me, but his being there and being understanding of struggles I was going through was a huge benefit to me.

As I mentioned earlier, I told one boyfriend in college. I was working in a chemistry lab as a junior and was dating a graduate student. He had a huge impact on my healing journey with his support and kindness. He was the one who got me connected with the resources I so desperately needed. He drove me to SIA meetings when I was too scared to go by myself and even drove me to meetings when it was for survivors only and he could not attend.

He also helped me connect with the courage to seek help from a school counselor, which eventually got me into a therapy group for women who had experienced sexual abuse and assault; I describe this in the "Group Therapy" chapter. I can't imagine where I would be today without his loving support in my life.

Sharing with My Husband

I met my husband right before graduating from college. We had what I would call a "false start" while I was in graduate school, but reconnected again later and eventually got married after we had both matured more. I am fortunate to have a spouse who is very patient and supportive of me, my needs, and my healing journey. We have been married for over twenty years, and I credit much of my success in my healing to his support.

Not to say that our marriage has always been easy. When we first got together, things were rocky. I had done a great deal of work in individual and group therapy for the mental and emotional aspects of healing as a single person and a person dating. But what I had not done is therapy for being in a committed relationship.

While we were engaged, I went to a therapist who specialized in working with survivors of sexual abuse. She helped me recognize when I fell back into old protective patterns of behavior and helped me understand how to share my fears and express my needs with my husband. She helped me understand it was important to include my husband in my experiences, especially when we were intimate. It sounds logical when you hear it, but it was hard to get past the fear of rejection without having someone tell me I couldn't get what I wanted in intimacy with my partner unless I told him what I was thinking and feeling. And believe me, she had to tell me several times before it went from something I heard to something I integrated into my belief system.

My husband has been a rock for me on my healing journey. He can get frustrated sometimes when I am sending mixed signals or seem to change my mind about intimacy from one day to the next. But he never stops communicating with me, never stops telling me how much he loves me, and never stops believing in me and my healing journey.

Sharing with partners is a critical thing. To get your needs met and to have support on your healing journey, you need to share something about what you are going through and why. How much and what you share is up to you, but you cannot leave your partner in the dark and expect to be successful in healing.

Sharing with Your Partner

When you tell your partner, don't drop it as a bombshell right before one of you goes to work or when they just got back from work and are tired from a long day. The drop and run technique is a way to avoid the fallout of what you are sharing and not a way to communicate with the person you care about.

Once you decide to share with your partner, sit down by yourself and think through a plan for sharing with them. You want to make sure your needs are met, but you want to be respectful of your partner as well.

Below are questions for preparing to share with you partner. These questions are good to discuss with your therapist so they can work with you on how best to approach and share with your partner.

Ask yourself these questions and write your answers in your notebook/journal.

- How much do you want to share with your partner the first time you talk to them about your abuse? Know that you don't have to share everything about your abuse in one session; you can do it over multiple sessions. This can help to make it less overwhelming for you to share as well as less overwhelming for your partner to hear you.
- Where is the best *place* to talk with your partner where you will not be interrupted by anyone?
- What is the best *time* to talk to your partner when you or they are not too tired or frustrated or too busy to have a real conversation?

Other Sharing Considerations

You can ask to schedule time with them to talk about something important. "I want to share with you something important that happened to me in the past. When is a good time for us to sit down and talk without being interrupted?"

And when it's time for you to share, if you're uncertain it's still a good time for them, ask them before you begin, "Is this still a good time to share what happened to me?" What are you comfortable sharing? How much of your experience?

Your partner may have a lot of questions about who, when, how, and what happened. Be ready for them to want to know the details.

You can prepare yourself to say something like, "It is too painful to share certain details with you, but I still want you to know about what happened to me."

You may want to write what you need to share beforehand so you can read it rather than just speak from memory. Just let your partner know why you are reading, using words such as, "This is really hard for me to speak about, so I wrote it down to read it to you instead."

You can practice what you will say, or practice reading what you wrote, before you meet with your partner. Practicing can help you find the right words to express what you are feeling. It can help you identify things that might be harder or more emotional for you to share, possibly even things you might not be able to share the first time you talk with your partner.

You may also need them to wait to ask questions until you are done sharing your experiences. You might say something like, "You'll probably have questions about what I will tell you. It'd help me get through it if you can wait until I'm finished before asking questions."

Give some thought to how much physical contact you want while you are sharing with your partner. Holding your hand or holding you or hugging you while you are sharing might be too intense for them or for you. Or that may be just what you need to tell your story. Let your partner know upfront by telling them what you need. You can say something like, "This will be hard for me. I really need you to hold my hand while I share this," or "This will be hard for me. I really need you to sit over there while I share this."

Share whatever you need from them, and be as specific as possible. It's okay to ask for more than one thing! "I really need you to support me when I go to my therapy sessions. I need that time available to consistently get to therapy to heal."

Be ready to let them know what you are and are not comfortable with. "I understand you want me to do certain things that you think will help me heal. But I am just not ready to do ..."

Be specific and let them know exactly who you want to know about your story. "I really want this to be just between us for now. Please don't mention this to anyone or share my story with anyone else right now."

Planning Your Sharing

Ask yourself these questions and write your answers in your notebook/journal.

- Do you want physical contact with your partner while you share?
- What can you share about your healing journey plans with your partner so they know what you will do to help yourself?

What do you want from your partner in response to sharing your experiences immediately and going forward? Do you want them to just listen for now? To give you more hugs? Do you want them to go to therapy or SIA meetings with you?

- What happens if your partner wants you to do something you are not ready to do? What if they want you to go to therapy, join a survivors' group, share on social media a #MeToo, or confront your abuser or family?
- Who are you comfortable having your partner share your story with? Do you want it to be something just between you and your partner? Can they tell your friends, their friends, your family, their family? Can they tell just certain people?

Your partner may struggle to know how to support you during your healing journey. Resources are available to help them understand what you are going through and how they can support you. *The Courage to Heal: A Guide for Women Survivors of Sexual Abuse* by Ellen Bass and Laura Davis has sections specifically for partners to read. And sharing passages from the book that are powerful for you can be beneficial as well.

In addition, Laura Davis wrote a book specifically for partners titled, *Allies in Healing: When the Person You Love Was Sexually Abused as a Child."* After they read it, they might want to share passages from that book with you.

Also, speak with your therapist about if or when might be a good time for your partner to come to one or more therapy sessions. Your therapist might suggest having that first conversation with your partner in one of your sessions. They can help you decide if your partner's participation in therapy will be beneficial to your healing journey.

Confronting

MEMORIES OF MY ABUSE SURFACED as my grandfather was dying, and they turned my world upside down. I only remember seeing him one time while he was in the hospital for treatment, and that was briefly with my boyfriend, acting as a shield from my grandfather, in tow.

At that time, I wasn't even able to share my experiences with my family or friends, so there would have been no way to have the courage to confront my grandfather about the abuse. Not even with him dying and seemingly helpless in a hospital bed!

My grandfather was such a strong, imposing, militant figure that I got nauseous thinking about confronting him, to the point of having a full-on anxiety attack.

So in many ways, I had an easy choice because I did not have to stand up to him and try to hold him accountable for what he did for me. But not having a chance to confront him posed a challenge in moving on and healing from the abuse.

At one point in my healing journey, I was so angry with what had happened to me I considered traveling to the cemetery where he and my grandmother were buried. I fantasized about covering his tombstone with a big sign announcing to the world that he was a child molester so people would know what a horrible person he had been But I also didn't want to taint my grandmother's memory or embarrass her family (who lived in the area) with such a public pronouncement.

Unfortunately, the universe did not give me an opportunity to confront my abuser.

Confronting Your Abuser

Consider whether confronting your abuser is right for you. This is something that would be good to discuss with your therapist.

After considering the questions below and speaking with your therapist if you decide to confront your abuser, please be sure that you do so in a safe place and time and have your supporters with you, in person or readily available to you afterward. Your abuser is a person who hurt you before, so don't give them an opportunity to hurt you again.

Write your responses in your notebook/journal.
- Do you want/need to confront your abuser?
- What do you want to say to your abuser?
- How will this help you on your healing journey?
- What do expect from your abuser when you confront them?
- What will happen if your abuser does not react as you expect or need, such as denying the abuse?
- How will this impact other relationships in your life for those who know or are related to the abuser?

- Who do you have to support you in preparing for, during and after the confrontation?
- Do you want to consider legal action against your abuser? If so, how would this help your healing journey or prevent others from being abused, too?
- How many ways could confronting your abuser improve your life? How many ways could it negatively impact your life?
- Is there a chance your abuser could retaliate against you for your accusations? Are you prepared for the potential consequences?

CHAPTER 18

Triggers and Body Memories

ONE OF THE MOST CHALLENGING ASPECTS of my healing journey was learning to handle body memories and triggers. Body memories are a physical re-experiencing of the traumatic event(s) where your body and nervous system have the feelings and sensations you experienced during the original event. Triggers are things that bring back strong memories of the abuse, strong enough that you feel you are living through the abuse all over again.

Triggers can be sights, sounds, smells, physical touch, people, places, circumstances, or thoughts that remind you of the abuse. Seeing someone related to the abuse, or someone who reminds you of the abuser, even someone that has a physical trait of the abuser, may act as a reminder. Anything that reminds you of what happened immediately before or during the abuse can be a potential trigger.

These reminders can lead to powerful and instantaneous symptoms, like sweating; feeling anxious, fearful, or panicky; hypervigilance or avoidance; racing heartbeat; difficulty breathing; or intrusive images, thoughts, or flashbacks. Some survivors have symptoms of such severity and duration to be diagnosed with PTSD.

Some triggers are obvious, like seeing a report about sexual abuse, or reading about someone's #MeToo experience. Other triggers are more subtle. For example, my abuse happened in a small workroom in the basement of my grandfather's house. I felt like he trapped me there, and situations that make me feel claustrophobic can bring back those memories.

Why We Get Triggered

Our brains are constantly evaluating information, determining what needs to be rejected and what needs to be processed and stored as memories. When processing information, both explicit and implicit memories are formed. Explicit memories are focused on factual information, and implicit memories are about the emotions and bodily sensations that accompany the experience.

According to WebMD.com, triggers develop out of our body and mind's efforts to deal with danger. When faced with a threat, our brain stops some of its normal activities so that our body can deal with the threat by fighting, freezing, or fleeing.

The brain attaches details, such as smells or sight, to the abuse memories that then become triggers that can turn on your body's alarm system. Your body cannot tell the difference between emotional danger and physical danger. Encountering a trigger can switch your brain into danger mode, even while the triggers themselves are usually harmless in normal situations. The triggers might also bring back the sights, sounds, sensations, and feelings of the abuse in a flashback where you relive the abuse.[8]

Survivors of incest and other trauma survivors may have very strong triggering based on body memories.[9]

Understanding Your Triggers

Knowing your triggers can help you be better prepared to deal with triggering situations. The most basic approach is to avoid triggering situations whenever possible. So identifying what your triggers are is a critical first step. Keeping a journal or notebook of when you experience being triggered can assist you in distinguishing the underlying cause of the response. It may take many triggered events before you can recognize the specific sound, smell, circumstance, and other details.

My Triggers

I am triggered by body memories. When boyfriends would touch me in certain ways or touch certain parts of my body, I would experience flashbacks.

I sometimes struggle with these reactions when my husband wants to touch me in certain ways or places, particularly when it is outside of a longer bedroom experience and is a more casual, in-the-moment experience somewhere in our home. In those

---

[8] https://www.webmd.com/mental-health/what-are-ptsd-triggers#1

[9] https://www.psychologytoday.com/us/blog/workings-well-being/201708/heal-trauma-work-the-body

DENISE BOSSARTE

moments, I remind myself that my husband loves me and wants to be close to me, that the experience is not one of him taking something from me but of sharing his attraction to me and his appreciation of my body, and of his love for me. And that I can enjoy what the experience brings. It took a lot of hard work and plenty of time to come to this point in my healing journey, but I am happy that I committed to keep working until I could get to this point.

What to Do When You Are Triggered

When you are experiencing a triggering event, you can do several things, some mental and some physical; you can practice all of these in advance.

Mentally, you can remind yourself that:
- the physical reactions of a pounding heart and rapid breathing are not dangerous and will soon pass.
- your body is doing what it's supposed to do, protecting you from perceived harm, but you need to work on the sensitivity of the alarm system.
- these are only memories and you are safe.
- you survived and are no longer in that original abusive situation. Concentrate on your surroundings to ground yourself in the present.

If you need support, reach out to someone you trust about how you are feeling. See if you can talk with them about what you are experiencing, either face-to-face or over the phone. Try texting them if it is easier for you to write about the experience rather than talk about it.

140

Physically, you can pay attention to your breath, try to slow your breathing or count the exhales. You can sit on your hands, assume the Wonder Woman pose (https://www.harpersbazaar.com/uk/beauty/fitness-wellbeing/news/a36820/how-standing-like-wonder-woman-can-boost-your-confidence/), do a quick yoga pose such as Balasana (https://www.yogajournal.com/poses/child-s-pose/), go for a brisk walk, or engage in movement that will distract you from what you are thinking. Whatever movement is practical, what you are comfortable doing and that feels right to you, can help ease or end the symptoms. Explore for yourself to see what works best for you.

But what do you do if you cannot avoid the triggers?

During a triggered response, it is difficult to feel there is any way to escape from the situation and the accompanying, overwhelming emotional and body reactions. It is hard to remember positive things to do to help yourself when you are in the middle of the experience.

One way to compensate for this is to prepare a "trigger response" plan that you can use when triggered and to practice the plan before you are in a triggering situation. Explore what works for you to calm yourself and write it down. Put it on a laminated notecard that you carry in your purse or wallet or enter a note on your cell phone, including phone numbers to call when you need them. Whatever works for you, keep that information handy so you don't have to remember it when you are stressed.

Identifying and Working with Your Triggers

Note: the questions below might be triggering to some readers. This section is one to consider working through with the help of your therapist or mental health professional.

Write the answers to these questions and the discussion with your therapist in your notebook/journal.

- Can you identify what can trigger you about your abuse?
- Are there sounds, tastes, or scents that trigger you? What are they?
- Are there thoughts, emotions, or sensations that trigger you? What are they?
- Are there words or things that trigger you? What are they?
- Are there places that trigger you? What are they?
- Are there types of people that trigger you, especially ones that in some way remind you of your abuser? What are they? What is it about them that triggers you?
- Are there situations or anniversaries that trigger you? What are they?
- What triggers can you avoid? How will you avoid them?
- What triggers can you *not* avoid?
- What helps you when you are triggered?
- Can you build a plan for what to do when you are triggered? What will you do?

• C H A P T E R 1 9 •

Memory Issues

MEMORIES OF ABUSE are tricky things. In their book *The Courage to Heal: A Guide for Women Survivors of Child Sexual Abuse*, Ellen Bass and Laura Davis include a chapter on "Remembering" and a later chapter on "Believing It Happened." They present information on memory and traumatic amnesia, such as what I experienced in my childhood. They write about what it is like to remember—the flashbacks, and body and sense memories.

They share that each person's memories and how much they remember about their abuse will be different. It is not unusual for survivors not to have clear memories of exact instances of the abuse.

They describe how it is normal to have vague memories at first and then remember more about the abuse as you work on your healing journey. If you don't have clear memories of abuse, you may have to rely on a gut feeling that you know something happened to you, something not okay.

My Blocked Memories

For most of my childhood, all the way into high school, I blocked the memories of the abuse. What I experienced during that time was the terror of ever being alone with my grandfather, in any place or at any time. And also the gut feeling of him being a creepy, sneaky, gross, and scary person.

I couldn't pinpoint why I felt that way, but I knew I wanted to avoid interacting with him, particularly by myself, at all costs. It wasn't until his prostate cancer diagnosis, when he was weak and dying, that I started to remember things.

Remembering My Abuse

Once I started to remember the abuse, I only had a few memories about specific occurrences. But even without the memories, feelings of being different, of being worthless, unlovable, and full of shame had directed my life up to that point.

When I started remembering, it was devastating. A part of me was relieved that there was something to explain the agony I felt and disgust I felt about myself. A large part of me blamed myself for what happened. And for a long time, part of me thought I didn't actually "have the right" to consider myself a victim of abuse because I didn't remember more than a few instances of being abused.

It wasn't until I joined SIA and read Bass and Davis's *The Courage To Heal* that I came to understand only one memory of abuse, or even no memories, could be possible for survivors. And that my abuse was as real as any other person's.

Childhood Sexual Abuse Is Trauma

Surviving incest is traumatic. The trauma you experienced as a child can impact both your body and your mind. There has been a great deal of research about and investigation of trauma and its effects on war veterans, prisoners of war, battered women, and others suffering ongoing trauma. The understanding of PTSD experienced by trauma survivors, its impacts, and its treatment have grown substantially in the last few years.

I have read a great deal about trauma and PTSD to educate myself on the impact of trauma. I've learned how it can impact the normal process of memory development, and how your brain can function differently in your day-to-day life when you are a survivor of trauma.

The good news is all of this research is deepening and broadening the knowledge about how sexual abuse impacts survivors.

Working with Your Abuse Memories

Note: the questions below might be triggering to some readers. This section is one to consider working through with the help of your therapist or mental health professional.

The questions below were helpful to me for understanding what happened to me so I could process my body memories and my responses to certain places/quality of places and certain people.

I wanted that understanding so I could work through the fear and revulsion that physical intimacy could bring up for me. I wanted that understanding so I could learn how to deal with my fear and anxiety of certain places and people. I wanted that understanding so I could live the life I love without being held back by the past.

Write your answers to the questions below in your note-book/journal.

- What do you remember about your abuse?
- Who was your abuser? Was it just one person? Were they part of your family, or someone you trusted, like a teacher or pastor/priest/minister/nun?
- When did it start? How old were you?
- When did it stop? How old were you?
- Where did it happen? Was it the same place each time? Was it in certain locations, or at certain occasions or events?
- When did it happen? At certain times of the day? At certain times of the year, like holidays?
- How were you abused? Were certain parts of your body involved? Were there certain acts involved, like oral sex?
- Did your abuser do all the physical touching, acts, and manipulations? Or were you forced to touch and perform acts on the abuser?

CHAPTER 20

Forgiving—Letting Go and Moving On

FORGIVENESS IS A TRIGGERING WORD for survivors. Our culture wants us to believe that forgiveness means saying that something was not important, or that it didn't happen. That when we say we "forgive," we mean the wrongs are forgotten and no one is held to blame.

When I speak of forgiveness, it does not mean I deny the abuse happened. It does not mean that I deny the hurt and the damage were real. It does not mean that my abuser, my grandfather, gets a free pass as if he did nothing monstrous or life-altering to me. It is quite the opposite.

When I speak of forgiveness, I am not focused at all on my abuser or the abuse itself. Those things are true, actual, and will never be erased from my personal history. They are part of what made me who I am today. Those experiences do not *define* me, but they *influenced* my life path in many ways.

When I speak of forgiveness, I am talking about forgiving myself for any misplaced belief that I am to blame for the abuse.

147

Forgiving myself for any sense of guilt or shame about what happened to me. Forgiving myself means letting go of my self-image of a damaged and unlovable soul. Forgiving myself means I no longer let the hurt rule my life and define who I am.

Forgiveness has been a process for me. It is not something that came in a flash of insight that shifted me from blame and shame to freedom and joy. On my healing journey, I grew to understand who was responsible for the abuse—my grandfather—and who was responsible for my healing: myself. I cannot change the past, but I can change how I live my life in the present and future.

It took me a long time to discover my freedom from the abuse that was ruling my life, my thoughts, and my heart. To finally let go of the blame and shame that were chaining me to the past and keeping me living my life from that space of victimhood.

I base the cover of this book on this vision of freedom—breaking free from the bondage that I thought chained me to the past and blossoming into the person I longed to be.

What About Others?

Besides acknowledging who was responsible for the abuse, I also had to decide how to deal with the people in my life who I am certain knew about my abuse while it happened—my cousin—and those who could have known about the abuse: my parents and grandmother.

My grandfather also abused my cousin, and that is why she recognized my personality change from an outgoing, loving child to a shy and withdrawn one. For a long time, she was the only one I confided in and shared my story with. I put aside the small part of me that wanted to blame her for not stepping in to protect me or stop the abuse. I needed the support of someone who understood what I was going through.

As I grew older, I came to realize that she most likely had been as mentally coerced as me, as afraid of other people finding out. She was a teenager when she realized what was happening to me. I look back at where I was in my healing journey and realize that if our situations had been reversed and I had been the teenager, there would be no way I could have spoken out to protect her. I am grateful that my cousin was there to help me and be a mirror for me to learn how to begin my healing journey.

I also had to decide what to do about my parents, the ones who should have protected me and didn't. We have talked about the abuse over the years. Since my sister's "reveal", my parents have said that they did not know about the abuse. Given the nature of the abuse, which happened during the summer away from my parents' direct supervision, it was not unreasonable for them not to know.

When my personality shifted, they did what they could to try to find out what was going on with me. I was too afraid and ashamed about what was happening to me to share it with anyone, family, friends, or professionals. So how were they to know?

Once I began my healing journey, my choice was to either keep them in my life or to walk away from them because of what happened to me. I also had to decide how much of my life I wanted them to be a part of. They are good people and have consistently shown in both words and actions that they are people of integrity and can be trusted, and I wanted to continue to have a relationship with them. So I made the conscious decision that I wanted my parents in my life.

For me, it was the best decision I could have made, and I have never regretted it. The result has been the privilege to have my parents be two of my best friends through the years—engaged, loving, supportive, and a huge part of my life. I speak with them weekly and visit them whenever life and its busyness allow. I love my parents deeply and would never have had these many years of caring and sharing if I had blamed them and walked away from them.

The prosecution of former doctor Larry Nassar revealed that the parents were often in the same room when he sexually abused his patients. And in her memoir *What Is a Girl Worth*, Rachael Denhollander describes engaged, dedicated, concerned parents who were present in the room during her abuse who still missed seeing it happen. This information allowed me to understand how abuse could be missed by even the most literally present parents.

And finally, my grandmother. Of all the people in my life, she would have been the most likely to know about the abuse. I won't say it was easy or uncomplicated to decide whether to have my grandmother in my life. From what I learned, her husband abused (raped) one of her daughters and at least two of her granddaughters. How could she not have known the kind of man she was married to?

My grandfather was manipulative, controlling, and maliciously clever. I am not surprised if the family dynamics were such that my grandmother either didn't know or was forced to "not see" the abuse.

Again, I made a conscious choice to get to know and spend time with this blooming woman. After his death, she lived her life as the epitome of a grandmother: sweet, caring, engaged, supportive. My husband and all of my friends who met her were always jealous that this woman was my grandmother!

I never talked with my grandmother about the abuse like I did with my parents. I never asked her if she knew or what she knew. I never mentioned a word of it to her. I simply built my relationship with her as I would if they had never been married.

Why I Choose to Keep My Family in My Life

You ask how I could have relationships with people who knew, should have known, and could have known about the abuse? I did not build and maintain these relationships from acts of repression. I was and am in the relationships knowing full well what was known and potentially known.

But to me, the key questions for deciding whether to have these people in my life were: (1) Were these people I would want in my life if the abuse had never happened? (2) What would I gain by blaming them and keeping them out of my life? and (3) What would I lose?

This wasn't a head project, an analytical decision process coldly done weighing facts and potential outcomes. It was a deeply emotional and spiritual evaluation of what I valued about myself, what I valued in my life, and which relationships would nurture me and help me grow and which would not.

I was fortunate that my cousin, parents, and grandmother were the type of people I want in my life. Their involvement in my life has allowed me to engage in my healing journey and flourish through it. For that, I am grateful beyond what words can fully capture.

Considering Forgiveness and Letting Go

Work with your therapist on the questions below to come to a decision if forgiveness is right for you at this time.

Record your answers to these questions and your discussion with your therapist in your notebook/journal.

- Are you ready to forgive yourself for the abuse that happened to you?
- If you are not ready, what actions do you think you can take to move you into and through this process of forgiveness? Hopefully this book, and all the chapters you've read prior to this one, give you lots of starting answers!
- What support will you need from family, friends, and professionals during this forgiveness process?
- Who are those people who will hamper or limit your healing journey? Who do you need to let go from your life?
- Which people who are already in your life will support your healing journey?
- Who else do you need to bring into your life on your healing journey?

The Good Stuff

I DID NOT PLAN OUT MY HEALING JOURNEY when I started. I moved through my life as a seeker, driven by a need to be free from my emotional pain and mental anguish. Along the way, I started to find the things that brought me joy, peace, and equanimity. My healing first came in spurts of conscious action followed by periods of unconscious reaction. But as I identified the activities, practices, and experiences that supported, enriched, and assisted my healing, I began to take note of the changes they brought and began including them as an ongoing part of my self-care.

Rather than reacting to each situation from a place of victimhood and from seeing myself as unlovable and worthless, I started to realize and own my self-worth. I started to believe in my goodness, my value, and my ability to love and be loved in a healthy way.

I learned to set boundaries for what was acceptable behavior from other people and what was acceptable behavior from myself. I didn't want to live my life spilling out from that dark past of abuse, but to live from a place of light where I would be the one responsible for my actions and choices.

It was incredibly hard to hold up a mirror to myself and ask if this was what I wanted from my life, how I wanted to live my life. I did that repeatedly as I struggled to find a balance between encouraging my growth and being overly critical for the times I didn't think I measured up.

As an extreme perfectionist, it was difficult not to beat myself up and shovel on a whole heap of guilt when I was less than I wanted to be at that moment. I knew guilt well; I'd been marinated in it, and shame, for years. But learning how to step away from the need to beat myself up was something that took time and focused effort. I needed to move away from beating myself up for the abuse and then avoid beating myself up for not healing fast enough!

Healing Is a Process

As you've read, my healing journey has not been one of steady forward progress, either. It feels like it is a series of steep climbs followed by various durations of plateaus. Sometimes the plateaus have lasted long enough that I feel I have "finally gotten over" the abuse completely. And then something will come along and shake up my world and show me there is an opportunity for more healing, more freeing.

These moments used to make me very angry. Having done "all this work" and then experiencing something that threw me back to having those same desperate, denigrated feelings again felt so unfair. But each time the recovery was faster and the healing deeper as I worked to include my self-care elements to support myself.

My life is not a ride of total bliss every moment. I still have times of fear, anxiety, and doubt. But these are responses to things coming from outside myself and not a response to how I let the abuse define me.

I now work to see these moments as opportunities to let go of more things that do not serve me. I don't view these as times when I am stepping back on my healing journey, moving backward rather than forward. I embrace these more as times when another piece of myself gets the opportunity to lay down a burden it had been carrying. It's like cleaning out a cluttered room and opening a window to let fresh air in. Nothing is ever "all or none" on a journey to yourself, but one of constant discovery and openings to better knowing.

My life has been one of learning, growing, expanding, and appreciating. I look back at the times when I was young when I thought it would be better if I were dead, and am so grateful that something inside me demanded I fight. I am grateful that as I stumbled my way along, finding the practices and activities that nurtured me along my healing journey, I never gave up.

Sometimes I wanted to give in and walk away from anything that challenged me to change, to stretch, and to release aspects of myself that no longer served me. It was incredibly hard work to commit time and energy to my healing rather than sitting in the pain, despairing of things getting better.

It took a long time and a great deal of work to realize that I was the one in control of my life; the past, my abuser, and the abuse could only control me if I let them. It was when I realized that it was my choice to live my life for myself, to move toward a future I wanted rather than running in fear from the past, that I could embrace what life offered me.

Family, friends, and companions have enriched my life in a way that would not have been possible if I hadn't stepped away from the hold the past had on me and focused instead on what I wanted now and in the future. Healing from and letting go of the past means that I now have the energy to put into doing the things I love and into being the person I am proud to be.

Your Healing Journey

Write your answers to the questions below in your notebook/journal.

- What have you learned about healing journeys in reading this book?
- Which of the practices I have shared do you think you can try for yourself?
- Imagine yourself healing and blossoming into the Thriver you can be. What would that look like?
- What can you let go in your life that does not serve you, starting today?
- What can you do for your healing journey, starting today?

Part IV:
POETRY JOURNAL

No More Secrets,
No More Fear

These poems were a way for me to express the emotions that were coming up related to the abuse memories. No rhymes for me, just my lyrical voice put onto paper.

DENISE BOSSARTE

CHAPTER 22

Journaling

THE POEMS IN PART IV are the ones I wrote after I started taking yoga classes while living in Florida.

The poems started out specifically about the abuse experience, but then moved through my coping with the abuse, then eventually concentrated on all the good things in my life, including myself!

I realize now that when I created my poetry chapbook years ago, a hidden spark ignited to someday publish them so that they could help others see how their lives could change on a healing journey. Not just talk about the fact things could change, but to actually show it!

In putting together this book, I revisited all of my poems from that time and did some editing. Several poems are as I originally wrote them, and others are a combination of poems to give the strongest voice.

I hope these poems inspire you to try journaling about your experience along your healing journey. Whether you choose poetry, a narrative, or just stream of consciousness writing it will be a tremendous aide to your healing journey.

Good writing!

WARNING: the content of the following pages has the potential to be triggering to survivors. These poems do not contain graphic content, but they do contain strong emotional imagery about my childhood abuse and also mentions suicidal ideation.

Please be aware of your self-care when considering reading the poems.

I: The UnNamed Fear

There is some terrible unnamed fear
that gnaws away at us even in the midst
of our joy, some cloud that hangs over
our heads or in the recesses of our spirit.
It is fear that keeps us from being whole.

~*The Chronicle*, April 2004
Christ Episcopal Church

DENISE BOSSARTE

Marred Canvas

My childhood: a watercolor painting,
your touch smudged and blurred,
your intentions acid on my canvas.

Bright colors lost, the fine details,
all the days, lost to your
urge to control and destroy.

All that's left are vague images
that build up to nothing, it seems,
but a lost childhood, lost memories—
yesterday's dreams.

DENISE BOSSARTE

All Sugar and Spice

Little girl's dreams:
Ponies and merry-go-rounds,
Pinwheels and cotton candy,
sugary-sweet, tootie-fruity treat,
Blow out the candles, make a wish,
May your dreams come true.

My dreams:
A nightmare that doesn't wait for the dark,
but catches me in shadows whenever I am alone.
Suffocating hands, demands,
you wear a face familiar to the Thanksgiving table
and 'round the Christmas tree.

Light bright the candles, no more wishing.
Stop my nightmares from being true.

Transformation

My earliest days—sweet and happy,
replaced by a long, dark night,
fleeing memory's pain

Ice cream floats with sugared treats.
Normal things children do,
turn to sawdust in my mouth

"Be a good girl. Do what I say."
Tricked into maiming my inner child.

Stains upon my soul today
and forever.

Wishes

I've wished I were dead
and fear would release its grip,
and trap my soul, no more.

I've wished I were dead
then I could escape your touch,
finally to be free.

I've wished I were dead
then my wounded, tortured heart
would find peace, at last.

Turmoil

I grip my skull desperately
between both hands,
twisting my hair and
pressing palms tightly together.

I will not let the turmoil
break free, or it will consume me.

My breath comes short and sharp,
Through gasping mouth, as the fear
in my heart grows stronger.

Emptiness looms then fills my being,
even as my head pounds
and my heart races.

I say a silent prayer.
A plea to make it stop,
to help me be free of that fear
I cannot name.

I sob and cry in silence,
with wide, dry eyes,
seeing nothing.

Body cramped and curled,
to ward off the blows
my soul and mind will feel.

The Drive

He is meeting mother half-way,
picking us up for a summer's visit.

Terrified, lacking confidence,
without the slim hope
that my sister's presence
would be enough to protect me
while we travel.

I know it will not be enough,
once we arrive.

Better Choice

I feel my skin as a foreign layer,
a thickened hide
that suffers your touch.
I carry it about me, thin protection
from your poisoned touch.

My insides are raw,
Tears and pain scratching
and scraping my heart,
until it bleeds from ravaged wounds
of sorrow and loss

Rescue me! Save me from myself!
Why can't anyone hear me?
Hear this voice that echoes
loudly in my head!

I feel like I'm going insane;
better than remembering.
I feel like I'm going insane—
it's better than facing you.

Sweet Dreams

Sleeping, breathing.
Ordinary things are difficult
when fear rules your heart.

Wariness lives in my mind,
telling me to beware of you.

Each night whispers a warning
at the edge of my sleeping mind:
"Beware! He's coming!"

What peace is there in sleeping
when nightmare's demons prey on
souls in daylight?

Fear echoes in my heart,
it whispers to a child's mind,
keeping me awake.

The tick of the clock
keeps time with my beating heart.
Night's terrors hover near.

Opening door creaks,
feet shuffle on wooden floors.
A monster creeps into the room,
intent on devouring my innocent heart.

DENISE BOSSARTE

You enter my room
and like a pine coffin
the walls close in on me.
I'm trapped, with no escape.

There is no safety here.
Out of sight means easy
victim to your ongoing lust.

Hands that hurt, not heal.
Strong arms that give me pain,
not the love I crave.

II: The Others

"Oh, Mama, just look at me
one minute as though
you really saw me."

~Emily, from *Our Town*
by Thornton Wilder

Can They Tell?

No, nothing's wrong—
Right as Rain,
Peachy Keen,
High as a Kite ...
(can they tell I'm lying?)

Why

Why did you let it happen?
Why did you do nothing?

Why didn't you
see it, hear it,
feel it, *know* it?

Why didn't you stop it?
Stop him?
Protect me?

Deep inside yourself
you *knew* he was evil

Knew what he was capable of,
what he had done, was doing.

Why did you wrap it up?
Hide it away?
Make it cottony soft
and perfumed sweet?

When did you decide
I was a suitable
sacrifice
in exchange for your
illusions of a *normal* life?

When did you convince
yourself I wasn't worthy
of protecting? of saving?

You had *me*
convinced too.

And Where Were You?

Where were you, grandmother
While your husband devoured me as a child?

And where were you, mother
While your father destroyed my soul?

Where were you, sister
Living blissfully, obliviously?

And where were you, my dear cousin
Fighting for your own redemption?
And you, my mother's sister
Drowning childhood ghosts in alcohol?

And where was I?
Alone with fate,
Abandoned in the dark.

Decimated

Sisters sharing secrets while playing in our room—
mine the kind that get packed away into closets,
hoping to be forgotten in the clutter
and dust of discarded items.

My sister can't imagine what I've whispered
into her innocent ears could be true,
and with the wisdom of a child
runs to tell my mother.

I sit still and silent in our room,
waiting for her to return,
which she does triumphantly,
and in a sing-song voice of victory
she tells me that "Mother says it isn't so!"

She turns back to playing with her Barbies,
Content with her world, not realizing
that she has destroyed mine.

Family Bonds

When a family's trust is broken,
children become the wreckage.
Now, what can we believe in?

Where to place the blame?
Feeling there was something
wrong with me, not him.

Who's to blame?
"Not you," they say from the outside,
but the child inside knows
only Bad Girls are punished.

The Snare

The dread rises from my heart.
Knowing rationally there is
nothing I can do. Sometimes
even accepting that as truth.

But it is often hard not to respond
to the hurt and pain, to try to give
enough love to help.

The catch is there is danger in helping—
like trying to rescue someone caught
in a raging river where the torrent
can sweep you away at any moment,
engulfing you.

The safest thing to do, the only thing to do,
is to throw out a life preserver,
point out the shore and walk away.

Where Am I?

To the point I am so wrapped up in Them,
in trying to please Them and the Voice
that I lose myself—

I can't think, I can't feel,
I can't act as I want,
as I need ...

to give and receive love as I see fit,
within the boundaries I choose.

God! To exorcise the Voice,
to release the burden, the chains
that bind me, confine me,
drag down my spirit and damage my soul.

To be free to live unfettered
by other people's expectations,
to be free to live as I choose—
as me.

III: Awareness

The longest journey of any person
is the journey inward.
~Dag Hammarskjöld

The Fire

A fire rages, exploding my eyes,
incinerating my heart,
shrinking my soul

like plastic under
its heat into a hard lump
devoid of color
or distinction,

my ability to feel
melting like wax
to form a shapeless
mass in my gut,

as the flames continue
to destroy what's
left of me.

DENISE BOSSARTE

The Strength

The questions haunt me,
echoing through my mind
in counterpoint to the pain
that unsettles my life, my dreams.

I'm living a life of lies—
lies of success, of happiness, of joy,
of a sweet childhood and trusts fulfilled.

In truth, my inner child
hides in the darkest depths
of my soul—bearing mortal wounds
but clinging to this shell
of an adult with unfathomable,
unreasonable, hopes of redemption.

"I can't do this! I'm not strong enough!"
I scream at her, but she doesn't listen—
too wrapped up in the terror and
single-minded belief that salvation
lies in my unworthy hands.

I am awed by her stubbornness,
her belief in me, who finds nothing worth
believing in, within or without.

The Dregs

A few old "friends" of mine showed up today
and took me on a walk along the edge of insanity

Mad, crazy mad! Driven insane by your lust
that devoured my connections to reality,
by your twisted designs,
by your selfish indifference to my peace of mind.

Grief and anger—
directed at me, directed at you,
directed at those who should have
protected me, prevented your horror
from stealing a child's joy
and returning only pain,
prevented you from coloring
my world in a heart's black and blue
and a soul's gray.

Look what you've done to me
with your hurtful hands—
Who would want me now?

Look what you've done to me
with all your demands—
Who would love me now?

Burden

I carry with me loneliness,
a ghostly wall surrounding my heart

Being the perfect child,
so no one knows
what darkness lurks inside

Keeping my wants,
my greatest desires,
secret and close
lest they are twisted
and used against me.

Loneliness lives in my heart,
my one true, silent friend
jealously guarding me from pain.

Clown Faces

Too many mirrors distracting me
from reality—
which face to put forward,
now, today?

Each one a false pretense,
mask to my soul,
clown paints to hide the
sadness, the pain, the fear.

It's ironic that these clowns' faces
cannot bring laughter
to my inner child.

Having It All

You can't have it all—
believe me, I've tried.

It only lasts a little while
before it blows up in your face
and your life
comes raining down,
crashing around you.

Denying myself what I want,
what is good for me.

Must I choose between
keeping the peace and
keeping my peace of mind?

Before

Turn back the clock, turn back time.
I want to remember.
I want to see the child I was, before.

The child I might have been
before he stripped me of innocence,
of trust, of faith in goodness
and good people,

before he bound the chains
around my soul,
and caged my heart,
the keys lost with the
memories of who I was,
before.

Growing Up

Wanting to grow up as fast as I can,
to be big enough, strong enough,
to outrun you, to resist you,

to be big enough to make
my own decisions and choices,
to no longer to visit you
under my parents' command,

to walk away and never look back,
disdainful of your efforts to control
the child who no longer exists.

Scattered

My thoughts run scattered.
I try to gather them up,
but they are too quick,
too nimble for my
fumbling fingers,
slowed by sadness and grief.

Sweet memories are lost,
shrouded in childhood terror
finding them demands
a price too high to pay.

Locked Away

I box up the memories,
wrapped in brown paper,
tied with string.

I place them on a shelf
of a closet in my mind,
one of an endless corridor of doors,
some locked, some not.

I shut the door,
my hand hesitant on the key.
I can't decide whether I am
locking it in, or myself out.

With some regrets and much sadness
I turn the key and set the lock.

Before I can change my mind,
I turn and place the key on the
wall with the others,
hoping that someday Time
will open this door again for me.

IV: The Light Shines Through

Truth is within ourselves,
it takes no rise from outward
things, whatever you may believe.
There is an innermost center
within us all, where truth abides
in fullness, and, to know,
rather consists in opening
out a way whence the
imprisoned splendor may escape,
than in affecting an entry
for a light supposed to be without.
~Robert Browning

Sea Worthy

My heart is empty,
the insides scraped away
like a tree being carved
into a canoe—
raw wood exposed,
all splintery,
with jagged edges.

It will take some time
to heal, to sand smooth
the rough edges,
to add a coat of paint,
and become sea worthy.

The Weight

The weight presses on my heart,
and a heaviness fills my soul,
I'm feeling lost in the quiet of
the morning darkness,

I am not ready to face it all today.

Feeling so many things,
mixed all together in
confusion, hard to pick
and choose, to identify
specific feelings or
thoughts, to isolate
the cause of my melancholy.

I wait for the sunrise,
the warmth and the light,
to burn away the mist
clouding my heart and mind.

Just a few more minutes
in the sun and warmth
to catch my breath,
is all I ask.

The Bridge

I see you standing across the bridge
that separates us, waiting for me.

I feel the chains, so heavy,
binding me here to the present and the past.
I am caught- trapped between
my fear and yearning.

Fear that envisions
monsters rising from
the waters to devour
me in painful mouthfuls
if I dare to try to cross.

Yearning that envisions your
embrace, your passion
and your love met equally by mine.

Soft breath, gentle touch,
the things two-as-one share—
these most do I crave

Touch me gently, I beg you
lest you awaken
body memories of shame.

Cool Rain

The cool morning rain
carried by a playful breeze
collects on my glasses,

blurring my vision
to indistinctness and
turning my focus inward,

away from my eyes
and their constant
interpretations

to the sensual feel
of the wind and the rain
on my skin,

to my breath, and
the beat of my heart.

The cool morning wind
evaporates the tears hot on my face
and carries away the pain.

Release

Then ...
I don't live in my skin
but six inches below it,
separated from events,
distant from tactile sensations,
cushioned and disconnected
from the feel of his touch
and the revulsion it arouses.

Turns into ...
Fear of a man's hand
carried with me, his
shadow swallows yours
as you reach for me,
innocent of intent.

Now ...
With patience and understanding,
you return again and again.
Always the same gift,
always the same open heart,
until your heart's warmth, and
your love, banishes the shadows
and I rise to meet you.

Moving

The furniture has been
moved out, all the knickknacks
and mementos packaged up
and sealed with tape,
each box carried out
one by one.

The empty floors have been swept.
Close the windows, lock
the doors, turn out the lights—
time to move on.

Working on It

Working on it,
chewing off the rough edges
until it's smooth enough
to stand on its own—
a mirror reflecting
my images multiple,
a magician's pool
telling a story fantastic.

Searching for beauty,
wanting the world to see me
so, dispel my doubts
Turning my search inward, I
find it waiting there for me

Dancing by myself in my mind,
breaking loose from the chains,
freedom found in the
music that touches
my soul and calls to
my heart's feet,
the rhythm is easy to find—
it matches mine.

The Beauty

It is difficult for
a caterpillar to become
a butterfly,

the pain of transformation
burning away the old,
providing fire
to forge the new.

In the end,
beauty is not in
the wings' colored
patterns, but with the
wings in flight.

V: My Heart Dances with the Stars

Wakan Tanka, Great Mystery,
teach me to trust
my heart, my mind,
my intuition,
my inner knowing,
the senses of my body,
the blessing of my spirit.
Teach me to trust these things
so that I may enter my Sacred Space
and love beyond my fear,
and thus Walk in Balance
with the passing of each glorious Sun.
~Lakota Prayer

Change

How have I changed?
No longer feeling raw and battered,
Filled with fear, pain and resentment.

No longer feeling cored out,
empty of hope, of feelings,
of love.

No longer feeling
like a diseased-riddled leper,
worthless and ashamed.

No longer focused on what people
see in me, think of me.

No longer full of false bravado,
of "Fuck you!
I don't care what you think
'cause I'm better than you!,"
when I feel the exact opposite inside.

How have I changed?

Now feeling part
of the world, not running from it.

Now I don't worry,
I never think about

what other people see
in me or don't.

Now feeling
confident,
proud of Me
and the freedom
I've won.

Now feeling happy,
joyful, filled with laughter.
Feeling peace, contentment
And love.

Now I just live
in joy, peace, and happiness,
centered and calm
as I go about my life
being me.

More Than Me

I want to See
I want to Be
less than myself
more than myself.

In your arms, at your feet,
Your touch secures me,
anchors me, awakens my senses,

my desires rise
under your sweet
touches, your fingertips
softly brushing my skin
whispering my name ,

I grow old with you
in that moment,
look back at all I have been
see all I am yet to become

and realize my place,
here and now,
is with you.

Closed Doors

I am not afraid
of closed doors anymore.

Doors closed to muffle
the sounds of you
playing computer games late at night,
Three-way calling with your friends.

Doors closed to soften
our laughter so
as not to waken
my visiting family asleep on the
sleeper-sofa downstairs.

Doors slightly ajar
to give kitty freedom
of access to our room.

No shame in our being together,
in our lovemaking.

No need to hide,
with our love.

Doesn't Matter

It doesn't matter
where I go or when,

I carry you with me,
tucked in a corner
of my heart,

your quiet presence
a comfort, providing
a peaceful stillness
throughout the tumult
of the day.

Knowing you
are there, knowing your
love is waiting for me,

ready for me whenever I
need its strength,
keeps me safe,
keeps me sane.

Wonder

I stare at the ring
on my finger
and am amazed
at what you could
see in me,
that you could
believe in me.

Knowing what you
knew about me,
you still wanted me,
needed me,
loved me
as I was.

Bedtime Stories

I awaken as you slip into bed,
late night for you, early morning for me.
You whisper to me the events of the day,
future plans, random dreams,
and silly thoughts.

Something you say tickles us,
rubs our funny bones,
and we giggle and laugh,
encircled in each other's arms.

Spooning together,
my hand warm on your thigh.
My feet and hands are freezing
during the day,
but turn to furnaces at night.
Yours are the opposite;
complement to mine.

Legs entwined at
the foot of the bed,
your feet cold, mine warm—
together they find a balance.

Breath's Caress

My head rests against your
cheek as your breath
washes over my face,
caressing my nose and
mouth, the smell of
you filling my lungs.

My heart bathes in your heart's light,
each reaching, finding matching songs,
giving and getting heart's delight

You're speaking to me
with lips closed firm and
eyes sleepy-shut.

I breathe you in deep,
your essence mingling with mine—
I breathe us out
together.

Resources

A NUMBER OF RESOURCES can be found online for survivors of sexual abuse. Each organization below has multiple resources to support the healing process of survivors. It is worth visiting these organizations' websites to explore what resources and materials are available from each.

I am providing these links as a convenience and the inclusion of a link on this list does not imply endorsement. These are just a sampling of the sites that can be explored. Internet searching is bound to turn up other helpful sites for your healing journey!

Books
By Ellen Bass and Laura Davis
- *The Courage to Heal: A Guide for Women Survivors of Sexual Abuse*
- *Beginning to Heal: A First Book for Men and Women Who Were Sexually Abused As Children*

By Laura Davis
- *The Courage to Heal Workbook: A Guide for Women and Men Survivors of Child Sexual Abuse*
- *Allies in Healing: When the Person You Love Was Sexually Abused as a Child*

By Harriet Lerner, PhD
- *The Dance of Anger: A Woman's Guide to Changing the Patterns of Intimate Relationships*

- *The Dance of Intimacy: A Woman's Guide to Courageous Acts of Change in Key Relationships*

By Brené Brown

- *I Thought It Was Just Me (but it isn't): Making the Journey from "What Will People Think?" to "I Am Enough"*
- *The Gifts of Imperfection: Let Go of Who You Think You're Supposed to Be and Embrace Who You Are*
- *Daring Greatly: How the Courage to Be Vulnerable Transforms the Way We Live, Love, Parent, and Lead*
- *Rising Strong: How the Ability to Reset Transforms the Way We Live, Love, Parent, and Lead*
- *Braving the Wilderness: The Quest for True Belonging and the Courage to Stand Alone*

By HeatherAsh Amara

- *Warrior Goddess Training: Become the Woman You Are Meant to Be*
- *The Warrior Goddess Way: Claiming the Woman You Are Destined to Be*
- *The Warrior Heart Practice: A Simple Process to Transform Confusion into Clarity and Pain into Peace*

By Linda Graham, MFT

- *Resilience: Powerful Practices for Bounding Back from Disappointment, Difficulty, and Even Disaster* by Linda Graham, MFT
- *Bouncing Back: Rewiring Your Brain for Maximum Resilience and Well-Being* by Linda Graham, MFT

By Various Authors

- *It Wasn't Your Fault: Freeing Yourself from the Shame of Childhood Abuse with the Power of Self-Compassion* by Beverly Engel, LMFT

- *What is a Girl Worth: My Story of Breaking the Silence and Exposing the Truth about Larry Nassar and USA Gymnastics* by Rachael Denhollander
- *Fighting Back: What an Olympic Champion's Story Can Teach Us about Recognizing and Preventing Child Sexual Abuse – and Helping Kids Recover* by Kyla Harrison, Cynthia S. Kaplan, PhD, and Blaise Aguirre, MD.
- *Everyday Resilience: A Practical Guide to Build Inner Strength and Weather Life's Challenges* by Gail Gazelle, MD
- *Resilient: How to Grow an Unshakable Core of Clam, Strength, and Happiness* by Rick Hanson, PhD
- *The Art of Healing from Sexual Trauma: Tending Body and Soul through Creativity, Nature, and Intuition* by Naomi Ardea.
- *Victims No Longer: The Classic Guide for Men Recovering from Sexual Child Abuse* by Mike Lew.

Meditation Instructors

- Jon Kabat-Zinn https://www.mindfulnesscds.com developed mindfulness-based stress reduction (MBSR).
- Thich Nhat Hanh https://plumvillage.org focuses on mindfulness, happiness, and peace.
- Pema Chödrön https://pemachodronfoundation.org is a well-respected Buddhist spiritual teacher and a bestselling author with practical and deep teachings on mindfulness.
- Deepak Chopra https://chopra.com is one of the leading mind-body-spirit teachers and authors. He

teaches on the benefits of incorporating meditation and a healthy lifestyle for increasing inner happiness.

- Tara Brach https://www.tarabrach.com is an author and teacher of meditation, emotional healing, and spiritual awakening.
- Susan Piver https://susanpiver.com is an author and meditation expert. She is the founder of the Open Heart Project, an online community offering meditation, courses, and support.
- Sharon Salzberg https://www.sharonsalzberg.com is an author and teacher of Buddhist meditation practices. She is the cofounder of the Insight Meditation Society (IMS).
- Jack Kornfield https://jackkornfield.com/ is an author and teacher of Buddhist meditation practices. He is the cofounder of the Spirit Rock Meditation Center.
- David A. Treleaven https://davidtreleaven.com/ is an author and trauma professional. His work on trauma-sensitive mindfulness is insightful.

Meditation Apps

- Insight Timer
- Calm
- Headspace
- Aura
- Smiling Mind
- 10% Happier
- Inscape
- Stop, Think & Breathe

- Buddhify
- Simple Habit
- Sattva

Resources for Survivors

These resources are provided for your convenience and information. I do not endorse, nor am I responsible for, the content of these external sites. Please use these resources at your own discretion.

67 Resources for Sexual Assault Survivors Who Aren't Sure Where to Turn

https://greatist.com/live/sexual-assault-survivor-resources
Although the title of the article states "Sexual Assault," resources available for survivors of sexual abuse are listed as well as those for sexual assault.

Survivors of Incest Anonymous (SIA) – 12-step program
https://siawso.org/
"A spiritual, self-help program of women and men, 18 years or older, who are guided by a set of 12 Suggested Steps and 12 Traditions, along with our Slogans and the Serenity Prayer."

Male Survivor
https://www.malesurvivor.org
"Helping inform, encourage, and empower male survivors and their loved ones to make progress on the healing journey."

ASCA – Adult Survivors of Child Abuse

http://www.ASCAsupport.org

"Support program designed specifically for adult survivors ... The two basic components of the ASCA program are individually reading and working the **Survivor to Thriver** manual *and* participating in ASCA meetings."

RAINN | Rape, Abuse and Incest National Network

https://centers.rainn.org/

https://www.rainn.org/about-national-sexual-assault-telephone-hotline

National Association of Adult Survivors of Child Abuse

http://www.naasca.org/

"[NAASCA has] a single purpose ..., to address issues related to childhood abuse and trauma ... offering hope and healing through numerous paths, providing many services to adult survivors of child abuse and information for anyone interested in the many issues involving prevention, intervention and recovery."

NAASCA offers a recovery page and a resources page with articles and links to sites to support survivors, families, and parents of abused children. They also have a talk show, "Stop Child Abuse Now," a newsletter, a blog, a YouTube channel, and Facebook sites.

metoomvmt.org

https://metoomvmt.org/

"The 'me too' movement supports survivors of sexual violence and their allies by connecting survivors to resources, offering community organizing resources, pursuing a 'me too' policy platform, and working with researchers to add to the field and chart our way forward. We believe that the movement begins with connecting survivors to resources for healing, justice, action and leadership."

Meetup.com

Search for Sexual Abuse Survivors groups and related Meetup groups for survivors. The Meetup groups are listed by locality.

The Allender Center – Evangelical Christian-based approaches.
https://theallendercenter.org/offerings/

"The mission of The Allender Center is to foster redemption and healing in individuals, couples, and communities by helping them tell their stories with awareness and integrity ..."

Dr. Dan Allender has written several books, including *The Wounded Heart: Hope for Adult Victims of Childhood Sexual Abuse* and *Healing the Wounded Heart: The Heartache of Sexual Abuse and the Hope of Transformation*. The Allender Center offers online courses, conferences, workshops, story groups, and Dr. Dan Allender's books. The Center has a social media presence on Facebook, Twitter, and Vimeo.

The Younique Foundation
https://www.youniquefoundation.org/

"We inspire hope in women who were sexually abused as children or adolescents by providing healing services through retreats, survivor communities, and online resources."

On the site's Faces of Survivors page, you can share your written story or video along with other survivor stories. You can learn more about the Haven Retreat and read their blog. Multiple resources for both survivors and their supports are on the site. They have a social media presence on Facebook, Twitter, Pinterest, Instagram, and YouTube.

Incest Survivors United Voices of America
http://www.isuvoa.com/index.html

"I.S.U.V.O.A. supports men, women and children that have suffered from the effects of sexual violence and child abuse."

ISUVOA has multiple resources available on their site. They also have a presence on Facebook, Twitter, Instagram, and LinkedIn.

Promoting Awareness | Victim Empowerment (PAVE)
https://www.shatteringthesilence.org

"Shattering the Silence with PAVE is a movement to create a world free of sexual violence and build communities that support survivors. We aim to empower students, parents, and civic leaders to end sexual violence with prevention education, promoting respect for oneself and each other. Additionally, PAVE creates a safe space for survivors to thrive after trauma."

PAVE has multiple resources available on their site. They also have a presence on Facebook, Twitter, and Instagram.

After Silence
http://www.aftersilence.org/

"After Silence is designed to help victims become survivors, and communicate in the recovery of sexual violence. Our mission is to support, empower, validate, and educate survivors, as well as their families and supporters.

"The core of our organization is a support group, message board, and chat room where victims and survivors come together online in a mutually supportive and safe environment."

In addition to the online interactive aspects of the site are helpful articles, book recommendations, and links related to sexual abuse and assault. There is also a Facebook site.

Help for Adult Victims of Child Abuse (HAVOCA)
http://www.havoca.org/

"HAVOCA is run by survivors for adult survivors of child abuse. We provide support, friendship and advice for any adult whose life has been affected by childhood abuse. HAVOCA was established in 2001 to provide support and direction to any adult who has experienced child abuse."

HAVOCA offers a blog, forums, book recommendations, links to organizations and services for survivors and advocates, and tools to find therapists and support groups. They also have a presence on Facebook, Twitter, and Pinterest.

Stop It Now!
https://www.stopitnow.org.

"Stop It Now! prevents the sexual abuse of children by mobilizing adults, families and communities to take actions that protect children before they are harmed. We provide support, information and resources to keep children safe and create healthier communities."

Stop It Now! offers Help Services such as a confidential helpline email, chat, and advice column.
At their Online Help Center, you find information relevant to your situation by selecting answers to one to three questions.

You can also connect with them on Facebook, Twitter, and YouTube.

Whitedoves Nest
http://www.whitedovesnest.com
"A site dedicated to survivors of sexual abuse and those that support them. This site provides stories, articles, inspiration and help to those affected by sexual abuse, rape and molestation."

This site focuses on presenting the stories of survivors which can be submitted under your name or anonymously. The site also contains an online Survivor Art Gallery, links to resources, and links to survivors' personal websites.

Pandora's Project
https://pandys.org/
"A nonprofit organization dedicated to providing information, support, and resources to survivors of rape and sexual abuse and their friends and family."

This site offers a message board and chat room, articles, testimonials, and multiple resources including links to organizations and groups helping survivors.

Thank you for reading my book! I invite you to visit my website at https://thrivingaftersexualabusebook.com/ to introduce yourself and read my blog.

It is my best hope that you found inspirations here to help you start your own healing journey or expand the one you are on. This book was a difficult one for me to write, but it was a heart project that I knew I needed to finish. My motivation was always how I could help other survivors by sharing my story of abuse and of healing.

My wish is for as many survivors of child abuse as possible to learn about this book so they can get the support they need for their healing journeys. And you can help me do that!

Please consider leaving a review on Amazon sharing your experience of the book at https://www.amazon.com/Denise-Bossarte/e/B00H2Y28HU.

Reviews are critical for potential readers to understand the value a book brings to them and also helps the wonders of the hidden Amazon marketing machine promote my book out to readers.

Please also consider leaving a review on Goodreads.com.

Book lovers are hunting for good books there, and you can help them find mine with a review.

https://www.goodreads.com/author/show/7524492.Denise_Bossarte.

I appreciate your honest review and guarantee that I will read each of them!

You can find more of my work and inspirations on Twitter and Facebook: @AmThrivingAfter, https://www.face-book.com/thrivingafter.

Please consider liking and sharing my content.

About the Author

Denise Bossarte is a poet and an award-winning writer, photographer, and artist. Denise is a certified meditation facilitator and contemplative arts teacher. She is an information technology (IT) professional working for a large urban school district. Denise holds a BA in chemistry, an MS in computer science, and a PhD in developmental neuroscience. And she is a survivor of childhood sexual abuse.

Denise spent her adulthood healing herself from the traumatic impact the sexual abuse had on her life. She is not a mental health professional. She is a Thriver who has traveled a healing journey and is able to share a personal, guided experience for readers to find and engage in their own journey to healing, to becoming Thrivers. As an unpublished manuscript, *Thriving After Sexual Abuse* was a quarterfinalist in the 2019 BookLife Prize Nonfiction Contest, Self-Help Category.

Whether writing on overcoming trauma in her nonfiction work or recasting her real-life experiences into award-winning dark urban fantasy in four novels—*Glamorous, Beginnings, Return,* and *Readings*—Denise tackles the dark side of things with courage, fearlessness, and compassion. Her self-published book *Glamorous* was a bronze medalist in 2019's The Wishing Shelf Book Awards in Adult Fiction, and her success with *Glamorous* earned her membership into the Horror Writers Association and the International Thriller Writers. Denise is also a member of the Nonfiction Authors Association and the Texas Association of Authors. Denise lives in Texas with her husband, Randy, and literary cat, Sapphira.